THE THRESHER TABLE

Celebrating the
First Hundred Years
of Bethel College
North Newton, Kansas

*Photographs, anecdotes and recipes
gathered and contributed by
alumni, faculty and staff*

Published by
Bethel College Women's Association
North Newton, Kansas 67117

CONTENTS

v   Preface

vi   Chronological table

viii   Introduction

1   Around the table: Photographs, anecdotes and recipes

105   Additional recipes and anecdotes

115   Recipe index

The Thresher Table Staff

Committee chair	Edna (Ramseyer) Kaufman
Copy editors	Ethel (Ewert) Abrahams Rosemary (Linscheid) Moyer
Photographs	Rosemary (Linscheid) Moyer
Anecdotes	Ethel (Ewert) Abrahams
Recipes	Louise (Duerksen) Koehn, chair Linda (Mueller) Kaufman Frieda (van der Smissen) Andreas Mariam (Penner) Schmidt Wilma Toews Maxine Will
Format	Ethel (Ewert) Abrahams, chair Carolyn (Mast) Schultz Rosemary (Linscheid) Moyer Marjorie (Hamon) Warta Eva (Geiger) Harshbarger
Editing	Monica (Dirks) Gross Carolyn (Mast) Schultz
Cover design	Mark Wiens, photographer Edwards Typographic Service
Graphic designer	John M. Hiebert
Publicity	Bryan Reber
Editorial consultant	David A. Haury

PREFACE

The Thresher Table shares some of the story of Bethel College during its first 100 years, especially as it relates to experiences which center around food. Photographs and anecdotes are arranged chronologically, with appropriate recipes interspersed. Additional recipes and anecdotes are included in a separate section of the book.

The Thresher Table committee was composed of alumni, Bethel College home economics instructors and dietitians, and representatives of the Bethel College Women's Association.

A general invitation was made in the *Bethel College Bulletin* of June 1984, welcoming readers to submit recipes, stories and pictures relating to their experiences with food at Bethel College. These contributions were supplemented by information gathered from college publications and resources. The committee edited the materials, eliminating repetitious stories and recipes. Recipes were largely retained as submitted and were not tested by the committee.

An effort was made to name the individuals on all except the larger group photographs. A short blank line in a photo caption represents an individual whose identity is unknown. Corrections and additional identifications are welcome and may be reported to the staff of the Mennonite Library and Archives at Bethel College, where most of the photographs are preserved in cataloged collections.

Wherever applicable, a person's relationship to Bethel College is defined as a graduate, non-graduate, faculty or staff member. A maiden name is given in parentheses followed by the married name. The year following a name indicates the year of graduation. Symbols used with the class year are:

> x   non-graduate, with projected graduation year
> A   academy
> AA   associate in arts (two-year) degree
> M   music certificate

Thanks is given to *The Thresher Table* committee members who served willingly and efficiently, to Waldo W. Leisy of Edwards Typographic Service for donating the cover photograph, and to the Mennonite Library and Archives for its services and use of resource materials.

Edna (Ramseyer) Kaufman

CHRONOLOGICAL TABLE

Signing of Bethel College charter	May 11, 1887
Cornerstone laying for Administration Building	October 12, 1888
First annual meeting of Bethel College Corporation	October 12, 1888
Dedication of Administration Building; first student assembly	September 20, 1893
Presidency of Cornelius H. Wedel	1893-1910
First Arbor Day observed with planting of 100 trees on campus	April 13, 1894
Organization of Bethel College Mennonite Church	Fall 1897
Installation of pipe organ in chapel	February 1902
Selection of maroon and gray as official school colors	1907
Groundbreaking for Carnegie Hall women's dormitory	June 20, 1907
Publication of first annual yearbook, *Echoes*	1908
First academy junior-senior banquet	April 1910
First presidency of Jacob H. Langenwalter (elected August 1910)	1910-1911
First observance of Founders' Day	October 12, 1910
Introduction of full four-year college curriculum	1911
First presidency of John W. Kliewer (duties assumed September 12, 1911)	1911-1920
Graduation of first college class	June 5, 1912
Extension of electric power line and water main to campus	1912
Accreditation of academy by North Central Association	1913
Extension of interurban car line from Newton to campus	1913
Construction of Alumni Hall	1913
First intercollegiate football game	November 14, 1914
First intercollegiate basketball game	1915
Establishment of home economics department	1917
First publication of *Bethel Breeze* as section of the Newton *Evening Kansan-Republican*	January 1918
Presidency of John E. Hartzler (duties assumed June 4, 1920)	1920-1921
Bethel Breeze renamed *The Bethel Collegian*	1921
Second presidency of Jacob H. Langenwalter	1921-1924
First homecoming day	June 6, 1922
Separation of college and academy	1924
Governance by administrative committee	1924-1925
Construction of Science Hall	1924-1925
Second presidency of John W. Kliewer	1925-1932
Academy discontinued	1927
Presidency of Edmund G. Kaufman	1932-1952
First annual booster banquet	May 1932
First meeting to organize Bethel College Women's Association	February 21, 1934
Addition of college dairy farm and equipment	Spring 1934
First spring song festival	May 27, 1934
Threshing stone adopted as official school symbol	November 16, 1934
Establishment of college post office	February 1935
First annual buffalo barbecue	1935
Accreditation of college by North Central Association	April 7, 1938
Incorporation of Bethel College campus as North Newton	September 1938

Cornerstone laying of Memorial Hall — October 12, 1938
Establishment of student co-operative boarding clubs — 1939
First banquet in Memorial Hall — May 7, 1941
First European exchange students arrived on campus — September 1946
Franz Shop erected — 1947
Presidency of David C. Wedel (inaugurated October 12, 1952) — 1952-1959
Dedication of Library building — May 1953
Cornerstone laying for Bethel College Mennonite Church building — October 25, 1953
Groundbreaking for Goering Hall men's dormitory — September 21, 1954
First Mennonite Folk Festival — March 1-2, 1957
Dedication of Women's Residence Hall (later Haury Hall) — October 13, 1958
Presidency of J. Winfield Fretz — 1959-1960
Presidency of Vernon H. Neufeld (inaugurated October 13, 1960) — 1960-1967
Name of annual yearbook changed from *Graymaroon* to *The Thresher* — 1961
75th anniversary of Administration Building cornerstone laying — October 12, 1963
Addition of wings to Goering Hall and Haury Hall dormitories — 1963
Dedication of Sand Prairie Natural History Reservation — October 23, 1965
Formation of Associated Colleges of Central Kansas consortium — 1966
Dedication of Fine Arts Center — February 6, 1966
Presidency of Orville L. Voth (inaugurated February 5, 1967) — 1967-1971
Dedication of Warkentin Court co-educational dormitory — October 15, 1967
Engagement of commercial food service for student meals — Fall 1968
Introduction of January interterm — September 1969
First Christmas banquet for community — December 10-12, 1970
First annual Women-Enrolled-at-Bethel (WEB) Day — March 26-27, 1971
Presidency of Harold J. Schultz (inaugurated October 24, 1971) — 1971-
First observance of annual Fall Festival — October 22-24, 1971
Voth-Unruh-Fast house moved to proposed museum complex prairie — 1974
Melting Pot of Mennonite Cookery published by Bethel College Women's Association — Summer 1974
Kauffman Museum relocated in prairie landscape — July 1977
First basketball game in Thresher Gymnasium — December 3, 1977
Wheat packaging enterprise initiated by Bethel College Women's Association — January 1979
Dedication and open house for Student Center — February 25, 1979
First National Conference on Faith and Learning — April 17-19, 1980
Open house for Campus Granary, storage and packaging facility for wheat weaving — September 7, 1981
Dedication of Kauffman Museum interpretation building — October 8, 1983
50th anniversary celebration of Bethel College Women's Association — October 6, 1984
Completion of Maintenance Shop building — January 1985
Dedication of Dobson pipe organ in chapel — February 22, 1985
Kick-off for centennial drive; Library addition groundbreaking — April 20, 1985
Inauguration of Kansas Institute for Peace and Conflict Resolution — November 1, 1985
100th anniversary of the founding of Bethel College — October 8-12, 1987

INTRODUCTION

A college centennial celebration is a once-in-a-lifetime experience. *The Thresher Table* is a part of that celebration.

How does one tell the story of Bethel's first 100 years? Perhaps no book could contain all of the history, with 10,000 living alumni scattered around the world, each with his or her own story of life at Bethel College. *The Thresher Table* attempts to portray only a part of that history—a kind of social history—that takes place around the table.

The "table" is an important symbol, replete with meaning. It is a visible symbol of the Last Supper, as Jesus gathered his disciples to share the bread and wine. In mythology King Arthur and the Knights of the Round Table gathered in the Great Hall for storytelling. The High Table in Oxford and Cambridge dining rooms is a symbol of prestige and is reserved for professors and distinguished guests. The Head Table at most banquets is reserved for program dignitaries. And the Thresher Table is a symbol of harvest time.

The Thresher Table has dual symbolism for Bethel College. In Bethel's early history many students and faculty experienced the thresher table on the farm, a table laden with food, as threshers in bib overalls gathered around to eat heartily and to share the stories of the day while women in print aprons hustled about carrying steaming bowls of food to appease the hungry threshers.

In 1934 all Bethel students became Threshers as the threshing stone was chosen as the official school symbol. Later the name of the college annual was changed to "The Thresher" and the athletic teams were called "Threshers."

One might ask: what are the events in a college history that take place around the table, and how can these events say something about life at Bethel College since its founding in 1887. In lifting out the significant events in the life of the college, it becomes evident that many of them centered around the table.

Among these are celebrative events: inaugural receptions, Founders' Day, Fall Festivals, Christmas banquets, spring flings, buffalo barbecues, alumni banquets and graduation dinners, to name only a few. At times the campus green became the table as picnics and barbecues were shared, and at other times the dorm room floor served as the party table. More importantly, the table marks the gathering place of the Bethel family for the daily routine of meals—a place to meet friends and to share the ordinary events of the day, a place to engage in lively discussions, and a place where food is both enjoyed and endured.

The table also marks a history of social customs, of where and how food was served. The dining room has been housed in at least eight different buildings on campus, including the historic Administration Building. The table recalls the time of formal dress with men in suits and ties and women in long white dresses, to the era of informal unisex dress with sweatshirts and blue jeans; from the serving of men and women in separate dining rooms to co-ed dining; from family style to cafeteria style; from a rather limited menu to salad bars and a choice of entrées; from solid oak tables with linen cloths and napkins to formica tables and paper napkins; from pressed back wooden chairs to bentwood chairs, painted many colors over the years, to chrome and molded plastic chairs. One constant remains, however, throughout the century—at meal times, outside the dining room entrance one can always find people standing in line.

The Thresher Table is a pictorial story of the Bethel family, its students, faculty, staff, alumni and the wider community of friends gathered around the table celebrating events, sharing stories and enjoying food. Whenever people gather to "break bread together," whether it is in the 1880s or the 1980s, there is more happening than the sharing of food, there is the sharing of one's self. *The Thresher Table* staff invites you to pull up a chair and join the Bethel family at *the thresher table.*

Carolyn (Mast) Schultz

AROUND THE TABLE:
Photographs, Anecdotes and Recipes

DATE WAFERS

Filling:

    1 pound dates
    1 cup water
    1 cup sugar

Combine in saucepan; cook. Set aside to cool.

Wafer:

    1 cup brown sugar
    1 cup butter
    ½ cup water
    1 teaspoon soda
    2½ cups oatmeal
    1½ cups flour

Mix in order given. Roll thin and cut into oblong pieces. Spread with filling or paste; place 2 together. Bake in moderate oven until firm. Ice with chocolate or white powdered sugar icing.

KATIE (GOERZ) KREHBIEL Ax'99

submitted by MARIAM H. (PENNER) SCHMIDT '25, faculty

Lodging for those who room in the main building amounts to $3.00 per term. No extra charges are made to these for fuel. Those who reside in the students' dormitory have to pay $5.00 per term and provide for their own fuel.

Board at the Boarding Hall costs $1.75 per week. The manager of the Boarding Hall reserves for himself, however, the right of raising the price from ten to fifteen cents, if the price of articles of food should go up.

Bethel College Catalogue 1895-96, page 14

Students ready for a picnic - 1890s

Men and women students on their way to the Boarding Hall - circa 1897

Changes which took place at Bethel's dining hall:

In 1915 men and women ate together in the dining room for the first time. Prior to that they ate separately—the women in the women's dormitory while the men ate in the dining room. The dining hall was located just west of the Administration Building where the Library now stands.

Students had their own napkins and napkin holders. Meals were served family style. The food was adequate but, of course, the students griped about it. I remember that eggs or bacon were rarely served for breakfast. Cornflakes, oatmeal, muffins, and sometimes toast, were the usual fare. Bread was usually home baked.

Jacob J. Goering A'16

Women students at mealtime in Carnegie Hall basement - 1909-10

A MAN'S WHEAT, OATS 'N RYE BREAD

2-3 cups bread flour	½ cup margarine or butter
1 cup rolled oats	2 eggs (reserve 1 white)
2 teaspoons salt	2 cups whole wheat flour
3 packages active dry yeast	1 cup medium rye flour
1¾ cups water	1 tablespoon water
½ cup corn syrup	4 teaspoons sesame seeds

Grease two 4x8- or 5x9-inch loaf pans. Lightly spoon flour into measuring cup; level. In large bowl, combine 1½ cups bread flour, oats, salt and yeast; blend well. In medium saucepan, heat water, corn syrup and margarine until very warm (120-130 degrees). Add warm liquid and eggs to flour mixture. Blend at low speed until moistened; beat 3 minutes at medium speed. By hand, stir in whole wheat flour and rye flour to form a soft dough. On floured surface, knead in up to 1 cup (more if needed) bread flour until dough is smooth and elastic, about 10 minutes. Place dough in greased bowl; cover loosely with plastic wrap and cloth towel. Let rise in warm place (80-85 degrees) until light and double in size, about 1 hour.

Punch down dough. Divide into 2 parts; shape into balls. Allow to rest on counter, covered with inverted bowl, for 15 minutes. Shape into 2 loaves. Place in prepared pans. Cover; let rise in warm place until light and double in size, about 1 hour. Combine reserved egg white and 1 tablespoon water; brush over loaves. Sprinkle with sesame seeds.

Heat oven to 375 degrees. Bake 30 minutes or until loaves sound hollow when lightly tapped. Remove from pans immediately. Makes 2 loaves! (High altitude: above 3,500 feet, reduce yeast to 2 packages.)

JACOB D. GOERING '41

PECAN COOKIES

1 cup brown sugar	½ teaspoon vanilla
½ cup shortening	1 cup sifted pastry flour
1 egg	½ cup broken nutmeats

Drop from teaspoon on buttered pans, placing half a pecan in center of each cookie. Bake in moderately slow oven so that cookies will dry as they brown. *Very good!*

JESSIE (BRAUNLICH) LANGENWALTER
submitted by a friend

STREMEL GURKEN
(Ripe Cucumber Strips)

1 gallon ripe cucumbers	vinegar
2 tablespoons salt	sugar
boiling water	2 teaspoons pickling spice
1 cup vinegar	whole mustard seeds
small onions	whole allspice

Peel cucumbers; scrape out seeds and cut into strips. Mix salt with cucumbers. Let stand overnight. In the morning, drain. Pour boiling water and 1 cup vinegar over cucumbers. Bring to a boil, but do not cook. Drain. Add a few small onions. Make a syrup with equal parts of vinegar and sugar. (If vinegar is very strong, use part water.) Tie pickling spice into small cloth bag. Add to syrup; bring to a boil. Pour over cucumbers; cook until cucumbers start to turn transparent (do not overcook). Pack into quart jars. Add ½ teaspoon mustard seeds and a few whole allspice kernels at top of each jar. Seal.

FRIEDA (VAN DER SMISSEN) ANDREAS A'13, x'17, faculty

College Day picnic - 1910-11
   Jacob H. Langenwalter A'00, president, is seated at left of center in front row with several other faculty members.

4

ROCKS

1½ cups sugar
⅔ cup butter
2 cups flour
3 eggs
1 teaspoon cinnamon

1 teaspoon cloves
1 teaspoon soda dissolved
  in ½ cup hot water
½ pound English walnuts
½ pound raisins

Drop on pans and bake in moderate oven.

EDITH (VON STEEN) RICHERT A'03
submitted by a friend

SURE-FIRE CHEESE SOUFFLÉ

2 tablespoons shortening
3 tablespoons flour
1 cup milk

1 cup grated cheese
6 eggs

Blend shortening and flour in saucepan; gradually stir in milk. Cook until sauce is smooth and thick. Add salt to taste. Cool slightly. Add grated cheese and well-beaten egg yolks. Beat egg whites until they stand in peaks. Fold egg whites into the cheese sauce slowly and carefully. Pour into individual molds or large dish; place in pan of hot water. Bake at 350 degrees for 25 minutes for individual molds, 45 minutes for large dish.

FRIEDA (VAN DER SMISSEN) ANDREAS A'13, x'17, faculty

Outdoor tea for summer school students - 1911

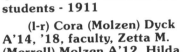

(l-r) Cora (Molzen) Dyck A'14, '18, faculty, Zetta M. (Merrell) Molzen A'12, Hilda (van der Smissen) Voran A'13, _____, _____, Laura M. Harms A'12, Helena H. (Gaeddert) Reimer A'12, Frieda (van der Smissen) Andreas A'13, x'17, faculty, Anna E. (Harder) Neufeld Ax'14, Bertha M. Unruh A'12

Mealtime in dormitory room, Carnegie Hall - circa 1912

(l-r) Zetta M. (Merrell) Molzen A'12, _____, Emma M. Linscheid A'13, faculty, _____, Maude C. (Krehbiel) Friesen A'15, Lena Mae Smith A'13, '30

One of the latest rules of the "Club of the Pines" is that a fine of a penny be imposed for the use of mixed languages in one sentence.

Bethel College Monthly, April 1910, page 15

A number of the students known as the "Club of the Pines" board at the Henry Martin home.

Graymaroon 1915, page 94

"Club of the Pines" boarding group at Henry Martin home - circa 1911

(back l-r) Peter D. Schultz '14, faculty, John F. Moyer '15, faculty, _____, Aaron J. Regier '12, faculty, Henry P. Peters '14, J. John Friesen '13, Jacob P. Baehr A'12

(front l-r) Ellison E. Martin A'07, John C. Dester A'13, Jacob S. Schultz x'15

A grip arrived from home loaded with chicken, wurst (summer sausage), coffee cake and pepeneet (peppernuts).

Echoes 1911, calendar: January 3, 1911

PEPPERNUTS (Pfeffernuesse)

3 cups white sugar
½ cup warm water
1 cup sorghum molasses
1 cup margarine, softened
1 teaspoon soda
¼ cup warm water
1 teaspoon cinnamon
1 teaspoon nutmeg

1 teaspoon allspice
½ teaspoon cloves
½ teaspoon ginger
½ teaspoon star anise powder
¼ teaspoon salt
7 cups flour

Moisten sugar with ½ cup warm water. Let stand overnight or several hours. Add molasses and margarine. Beat with mixer. Dissolve soda in ¼ cup warm water. Combine with sugar mixture. Add spices and salt to flour; mix. Stir into liquid mixture, adding more flour, if needed, to make a very stiff dough. Keep covered in refrigerator until convenient to bake.

On floured board, roll dough with palms of hands into ½-inch thick rolls; cut into small pieces. Place on greased baking pans. Bake at 300 degrees for 10-12 minutes or until golden brown. Makes about 5 quarts.

This recipe was used every Christmas by Helen (Isaac) Moyer who claimed that it was the peppernut recipe, with a few present-day adaptations, used by and passed on from early Bethel faculty wives, Helene (Riesen) Goerz, Jessie (Braunlich) Langenwalter and Lena A. (Krehbiel) Wedel. Mother liked to make these soon after Thanksgiving so that they could "ripen" for several weeks before Christmas. Our family uses half the amount of sugar suggested.

ROSEMARY (LINSCHEID) MOYER '52, staff

Men students from Mountain Lake, Minnesota, having a meal in dormitory room - 1911-12

(l-r) Peter D. Schultz '14, faculty, Jacob S. Schultz x'15, Aaron J. Regier '12, faculty, David H. Bargen x'15, Isaac J. Dick A'11, '13, J. John Friesen '13, Peter F. Schroeder x'15

DUTCH APPLE CAKE

2 cups flour
2 teaspoons baking powder (slightly rounded)
1 teaspoon salt
½ cup sugar
¼ cup lard or butter, melted
1 cup milk
1 egg

Sift dry ingredients together 3 times. Add other ingredients and stir to a smooth dough. Spread dough in well-buttered 9-inch pie pan. Pare 5 apples; cut into eighths, removing cores. Press sharp edge of pieces into dough in parallel rows. Sprinkle surface with sugar and cinnamon to taste. Bake in 350-degree oven until apples are tender. Serve with caramel or lemon sauce. *One-half of this recipe makes a large cake in a pie pan.*

MYRTLE (WATKINS) DOELL A'08
submitted by NORMA (DOELL) WALKER '35

WATERMELON PICKLES

Remove the outer green part from watermelon rinds. Cut into serving lengths. Let stand overnight in salt water, using about 3 quarts water to ½ cup pickling salt. In the morning, drain and rinse well. Cook in clear water until tender. Pack into stone jar or crock. Heat equal amounts of vinegar and sugar with a few pieces of stick cinnamon. Pour over rind. Let stand overnight. Drain and heat syrup again.

Pack into jars; cover with hot vinegar syrup. Seal.

MELTING POT OF MENNONITE COOKERY page 97

Watermelon "spree" in Goerzes' apple orchard - September 24, 1910.

Echoes 1911

A watermelon party - circa 1913

(l-r) Samuel F. Langenwalter Ax'14, _____, Albert L. Langenwalter A'14, _____

Thanksgiving Day Celebration

Thanksgiving Day at Bethel College was celebrated in a unique way. Usually a two days' vacation has been granted, but this year Thursday only was a holiday. It was made the occasion of a big college family gathering, in which the students were the guests of the faculty.

By one o'clock the students gathered in the gymnasium where they were received by the faculty members. Soon all were seated at the five long tables on which plates had been laid for 250 guests.

After the first course, consisting of turkey, had been dispatched, R. A. Goerz, as toastmaster, asked Professor Doell to respond to the toast, "Anatomy of Turkey." After this the ladies' glee club sang a selection, and Professor P. J. Wedel made a "Quantitative and Qualitative Analysis" of the crowd.

After the men's glee club had sung a song and responded to an encore, the second course was served. Then followed toasts by Professor E. E. Leisy on "Esprit de Corps," Irvin Haury on the annual, "Graymaroon," and Professor H. D. Penner gave some "Afterthoughts."

In the evening the college band of thirteen pieces made its initial appearance with a half-hour concert. Then followed two interclass basketball games.

Bethel College Monthly, December 1914, page 15

NELLIE GOERTZ CAKE

    1 cup sugar

    1 egg yolk, mixed with sugar

    1 cup sweet milk

    1½ cups cake flour, sifted with 1 teaspoon soda and ½ teaspoon salt

    1 teaspoon vanilla

    1 square bitter chocolate or 2 tablespoons cocoa (the chocolate must be melted with butter the size of a walnut)

Bake at 325 degrees in 9x9-inch pan.

MYRTLE (WATKINS) DOELL A'08
submitted by NORMA (DOELL) WALKER '35

Thanksgiving banquet in Alumni Hall - November 1914

    The academy seniors at far right table are dressed as pilgrims. Young children are seated at their own table in upper right.

RHUBARB DESSERT

¾ cup margarine   2 cups sugar
2 cups flour   4 tablespoons flour
5 cups rhubarb   ½ cup evaporated milk
1 tablespoon lemon juice ¾ cup sugar
6 eggs, separated   ½ teaspoon salt

Mix together margarine and flour. Pat into 9x13-inch pan; top with rhubarb. Combine lemon juice, egg yolks, sugar, flour and evaporated milk. Pour over crust. Bake at 350 degrees for 45 minutes. Cool. Beat egg whites with ¾ cup sugar and salt. Spread over fruit mixture and bake at 350 degrees until lightly browned.

HILDA (HAURY) GOERING x'35

Academy junior-senior banquet in Alumni Hall - April 24, 1915

College juniors roasting marshmallows over kerosene lanterns - 1914-15

(standing l-r) Gerhard Friesen '16, Irvin A. Haury A'10, '16, Arnold G. Isaac '16

(sitting l-r) Alfred Habegger '16, Helene (Riesen) Goertz A'10, '17, librarian, Marie S. (Wollmann) Lohrentz '16, faculty, Elma C. Schowalter x'16, librarian, Barbara (Hirschy) Habegger '16, Caroline A. Waltner x'16, Ernest E. Leisy A'09, x'13, faculty, Ralph W. Davis x'16

Unexpected Crowd at Picnic Supper
(College Day anniversary meal served on the south side of the David and Helene Goerz home)

More people were present than usually eat at the "hash hall" because all students and friends had been invited provided they brought their quarters, as Professor Moyer had announced in chapel. About 175 people were present, judging by the shortage of plates, of which there were only 150. The cheese sandwiches and the cups also gave out. This was rather a calamity since it necessitated the use of the same cup by several persons. However, since germs were not considered, it was a successful plan and no one had to do without a sip of hot chocolate.

The Bethel Collegian, October 18, 1921, front page

All buildings are lighted by electricity; city water is used in all dormitories.

Bethel College Catalog 1917-18, page 13

Brothers who prepared their own meals in the dormitory - 1915-16

(l-r) Edward H. Linscheid A'16, Alfred G. Linscheid A'16, x'21

MACARONI SALAD

4 pounds macaroni
⅜ pound celery, chopped
some peppers, chopped
1 ounce onions, chopped
2 ounces relish
2 ounces pimento, chopped
1 pound hard-boiled eggs, chopped
¾ ounce salt
1¼ tablespoons vinegar
½ pound salad dressing

Cook macaroni in salted water until tender; drain. Add remaining ingredients; chill.
College dining hall recipe.

MARIE (MIERAU) SCHMIDT x'32

OVEN-FRIED CHICKEN

    3-pound frying chicken, cut up
    ½ cup margarine
    1 egg
    ½ cup milk
    1 cup flour
    1 teaspoon baking powder
    2 teaspoons paprika
    1 teaspoon salt

Melt margarine on a cookie sheet covered with aluminum foil, shiny side down. Beat egg; add milk. Dip chicken in this mixture, then shake with dry ingredients in tightly-covered bowl. Bake at 400 degrees for 30 minutes. Turn; bake 30 minutes longer, for a total of at least 1 hour.

CYNTHIA (KLASSEN) GOERZEN '77, staff

A rabbit fry at P. I. Schroeders' February 3, 1913.

Echoes 1913

Senior Sneak Day

When I graduated from college in 1926, we had the custom of senior sneak day. No one but the seniors knew when that would be. But all of a sudden the other students were aware that there were no seniors in the classes. So they knew they had sneaked off somewhere for a whole-day picnic.

Marie J. (Regier) Janzen A'19, '26

Browsing through "Breezes" Bares Behavior of Bad Bethel Boys

The feature writer of 1918 describes the delightful escapades of his illustrious predecessors thus: "School life to them meant midnight spreads. To furnish these properly, nightly raids were made into the neighboring poultry yards, orchards and melon patches. Once, when they were seizing a chicken, it howled so unmercifully that the boarding house proprietor, who kept a fine flock of fowls, thrust his head out of an upper window and asked, 'Vas ist das?' The chicken had been affectionately hushed, silence was restored and no investigation ensued."

The Bethel Collegian, January 13, 1938, pages 1 and 3

Roasting wieners - spring 1919 *courtesy of* **Marie J. (Regier) Janzen A'19, '26**

Returning to the campus following a rabbit hunt - circa 1916

A page from home economics notebook of Helen L. (Isaac) Moyer A'09, '15, faculty

College and academy students at a party - 1916-17

(back l-r) Justina (Janzen) Tenhoff x'20, Henry J. Ewert Ax'20, Ruth E. (Hohmann) Moyer A'17, M'19, Abraham V. Tieszen A'14, '19

(front l-r) Henry A. Fast '17, faculty, Elizabeth S. (Linscheid) Guyer '17, Edward D. Schmidt '19, Wanda S. (Isaac) Tieszen '19, faculty

BLACK BOTTOM PIE

½ cup sugar
1 tablespoon cornstarch
2 cups scalded milk
4 eggs, separated
6-ounces semi-sweet chocolate chips
1 teaspoon vanilla
1 tablespoon gelatin
½ cup sugar
1 baked or graham cracker pie shell

Combine ½ cup sugar, cornstarch, milk and egg yolks. Cook. To 1 cup of this custard, add chocolate chips; stir until melted. Add vanilla. Pour into shell; chill. To the other cup of custard, add plain gelatin dissolved in ¼ cup cold water. Stir; chill. Beat egg whites with ½ cup sugar until stiff. Fold into custard gelatin mixture. Pour over chocolate in shell. Chill. Garnish with whipped cream.

WANDA S. (ISAAC) TIESZEN '19, faculty
submitted by KAROLYN (KAUFMAN) ZERGER A'46, x'50

TEMPURA (Japanese)

Prepare dipping sauce, fish and vegetables, and batter, in that order.

Dipping sauce:

 2 tablespoons (scant) light soy sauce
 ½ cup dashi or fish stock

Combine ingredients over heat. Bring just to a boil; keep warm.

Fish and vegetables:

 shrimp, shelled, deveined, tail on, underbelly scored
 fillet of white meat fish, lightly salted, bite-sized slices
 small whole perch or smelt
 onion, sliced in rings
 carrot, shredded, about 2 inches long
 yam or sweet potato, sliced ¼-inch thick
 eggplant, cut in wedges
 string beans, stringed, cut ½-inch long
 green squash, sliced ¼-inch thick
 broccoli, bite-sized flowerlets
 snow peas, tips and strings removed
 celery leaves, chopped
 fresh mushrooms, stems off, stuffed with seasoned
  ground meat
 green pepper, sliced

Arrange fish and vegetables attractively on large platter. Foods should be thoroughly dry.

Batter:

1 egg	1 cup flour
1 cup ice-cold water	⅓ cup potato starch
1 teaspoon sugar	1 tablespoon baking powder
pinch of salt	

Break egg into water. Add sugar and salt. Mix together flour, potato starch and baking powder. Add flour mixture to the liquid. Mix lightly with chopsticks (batter will be lumpy). Heat oil to 340 degrees. Pour hot dipping sauce into small bowls; add grated fresh daikon (large Japanese radish) and grated ginger. Dip prepared fish and vegetables in batter lightly and deep-fry. Serve with rice (foods do not need to be completely covered with batter.)

SHINGO KAJINAMI '66

Oriental banquet in Alumni Hall - circa 1917-18

(l-r) Anna Belle Dyck '23, Hilda H. (Wedel) Osburn Ax'17, x'21, Elizabeth K. (Linscheid) Regier A'09, '19, faculty, _____, Ruth L. (Kliewer) Liebenberg A'23, '28

I came to Bethel College in 1917 at the request of President J. W. Kliewer to organize a home economics department and to serve as dietitian for the dining hall.

During my term it was decided that both the young women and men should be served in the dining hall. A wall was taken out and the east part of the main floor of the Boarding Hall was made part of the dining hall. Thus, the basement of Carnegie Hall, which had been the women's dining hall, was made available for a foods lab. The equipment was ordered and we were set up for classes in the fall of 1917.

I taught the foods, clothing and home management classes, planned the meals and did the buying for the food service. I was fortunate in having very good, cooperative cooks and a group of loyal students as waiters. We had several good years together. They were hard years because they were war years and the students could not pay much. So, from that standpoint, it was difficult to satisfy them and to keep them happy.

Frieda (van der Smissen) Andreas A'13, x17, faculty

Foods: The purpose of these courses is to arouse in young women a greater interest in cookery. Emphasis is laid on marketing, the economical preparation and dainty serving of nutritious foods. . . . Students enrolling in these courses are required to wear white princess aprons of rather heavy material in the laboratory.

Bethel College Catalog 1917-18, page 68

Home economics class in Carnegie Hall basement - 1918-19

(l-r) Frieda (van der Smissen) Andreas A'13, x'17, faculty, _____, Esther R. (Mouttet) Nachtigal A'21, x'26, Elizabeth (Funk) Nickel A'19, Anna F. (Giffen) Keel Ax'22, Emma (Schrag) Stucky Ax'22

STEAMED PUDDING

    1 cup sugar
    ½ cup butter or oleo
    2 egg yolks
    2 cups bread crumbs soaked in 1 cup sour milk
    1 cup flour
    1 teaspoon soda
    1 teaspoon cinnamon
    ¼ teaspoon nutmeg
    1 teaspoon vanilla
    1 cup nuts, chopped
    1 cup raisins
    2 egg whites, beaten stiff

Cream sugar and butter; add egg yolks, cream; add soaked bread crumbs. Sift flour, soda, cinnamon and nutmeg; add to creamed mixture. Add vanilla, nuts and raisins. Add beaten egg whites and put into well-greased steamer pan. Steam 1½ hours. Serve hot with hard sauce:

    ¼ cup butter
    1 teaspoon flavoring
    ¾ cup powdered sugar

FRIEDA (VAN DER SMISSEN) ANDREAS A'13, x'17, faculty

COCONUT KISSES

2 stiffly beaten egg whites
2 cups cornflakes
1 cup sugar
½ cup nutmeats
1 cup moist shredded coconut
½ teaspoon vanilla

Beat egg whites and sugar. Add vanilla. Fold in remaining ingredients. Drop from spoon onto greased baking sheet. Bake 20 minutes in 350-degree oven or until lightly browned. Cool slightly before removing from pan. Makes 1½ dozen.

AVIS (UNRUH) BRANDT '65

ENGLISH TOFFEE

1 cup sugar   1½ tablespoons butter
¾ cup milk   ½ teaspoon vanilla or lemon flavoring
¾ cup light   pinch of salt
  cream

Cook all except butter and flavoring to 244 degrees. Add butter and continue cooking to 252 degrees. Add flavoring. Pour onto greased metal table. While still warm, cut into squares with knife; break when cold. Walnuts, almonds or pecans may be added.

MAMIE (KENNEDY) PHILLIPS faculty
submitted by LINDA (MUELLER) KAUFMAN '35

"Little girls" party in Carnegie Hall basement - circa 1920

(back l-r) Martha F. (Goering) Smith A'19, x'23, Ruth V. (Penner) Dirks A'18, Kathryne (Wiebe) Johnson x'24, Anna M. (Miller) Kaufman A'16, '22, faculty, Esther (Hohmann) Schuermann M'21, Anna Hohmann x'26

(middle l-r) Anna E. Staufer '28, Edna H. (Krehbiel) Young M'21, '24, Augusta Schmidt A'16, '22, Helen A. (Wiebe) Claassen x'22, Edna (Waltner) Gering M'21, Elsie (Martin) Latschar M'21, Ruth E. (Harms) Pankratz '24, _____, Minnie M. Harms '24, faculty, Anna (Enns) Siemens A'18, '22

(front l-r) Margaret (Dirks) van der Smissen A'21, Marie J. (Regier) Janzen A'19, '26, _____, Marie (Dester) Langenwalter x'24, Esther (Goering) Stucky A'20

*Freshman Tacky Party
Saturday*

Tin cans, torn newspapers and hobo costumes were sources of fun at the freshman tacky party Saturday night.

Most of the evening was devoted to stunts. The class was divided into three groups: "The Walton School for Criminals," "The Buhler Reform School" and "The Moundridge School for the Blind." The leaders were Clarence Spangler, Harold Regier and Sam Thierstein, respectively. Each group demonstrated its ability along musical and oratorical lines. Professor and Mrs. Doell acted as judges and announced "The Walton School for Criminals" . . . as the winner.

Refreshments consisting of fruit, meat sandwiches, cake, Eskimo pies and candy cigars were served at the close of the evening. Selma Flaming had charge of refreshments. Art Waltner had charge of the entertainment, and Edith Kuhns of the decorations. Helen Yergler and Sam Thierstein were given prizes for the best costumes.

Graymaroon 1929, page 35

Freshman-senior "tacky" party, Alumni Hall - 1920

CRUMB CAKE

    2 cups brown sugar
    1 cup butter, lard or shortening
    3 cups flour

Mix with hands as for pie dough. Reserve 1 cup of crumbs to put on top before baking. Add to remaining crumbs:
    1/2 cup sweet milk
    1/2 cup sour milk
    scant teaspoon soda
    1 egg
    1 teaspoon baking powder

Put in greased pan and place reserved crumbs over top. Bake at 350 degrees for about 25-30 minutes.

JESSIE (BRAUNLICH) LANGENWALTER
submitted by a friend

RHUBARB SALAD

2 cups rhubarb, diced
1 cup water
1 cup sugar
3 ounces strawberry gelatin
1 cup celery, chopped
½ cup nuts

Cook rhubarb in water for 10 minutes. Add sugar and gelatin, stirring to dissolve. Cool until partly congealed; add celery and nuts. Pour into mold and chill.

ANNA (ENNS) SIEMENS A'18, '22

PEAS DE LUXE

2 packages frozen peas
1 onion
1 can mushrooms
1 can water chestnuts
1 can cream of mushroom soup
¼ cup milk or cream

Place peas in boiling water. After they start to boil, cook for 3 minutes; drain. Sauté onion, add to peas with mushrooms, sliced chestnuts, soup and milk or cream. Heat well and serve. String beans may be used instead of peas.

ANNA (ENNS) SIEMENS A'18, '22

Home economics club - 1920-21

(back l-r) Anna M. (Miller) Kaufman A'16, '22, faculty, Linda E. (Kliewer) van der Smissen A'21, x'25, Elma (Richert) Crockett A'23, '30, Katherine Walde Ax'24, Kathryne (Wiebe) Johnson x'24, Hazel B. (Blatchley) Freeburg x'24, Esther (Goering) Stucky A'20, Ruth V. (Penner) Dirks A'18

(middle l-r) Anna (Enns) Siemens A'18, '22, Erna L. (Penner) Poirier A'22, x'27, Anna F. (Balzer) Ratzlaff A'24, Adeline (Schrag) Deissler '21, Dorris I. (Schultz) Penner A'21, x'25, Tena (Adrian) Balzer A'22, Elizabeth W. Nickel A'23, '48

(front l-r) Esther R. (Mouttet) Nachtigal A'21, x'26, Marie (Dester) Langenwalter x'24, Margaret Detweiler, faculty, Esther H. (Kliewer) Bargen '25, staff, Marie D. (Staufer) Regier, A'17, '21, Hilda (Schrag) Goering A'21

18

Bethel Students Working Their Way

Every spring the business office experiences a regular scramble for jobs by worthy and ambitious students who declare the college owes them a job for the next school year. Possibly the largest number of applications is made for work in the dining hall or kitchen where eight hash slingers are needed, also two dish dryers, two utensil washers and one superintendent of the dishwashing department. If a student particularly desires a more intimate acquaintance with the dining hall storeroom (always well stocked with oranges, apples and bananas), he will invariably apply for the office of handyman.

The Bethel Collegian, February 9, 1927, page 3

BUBBAT (Sausage Bread)

    1 cake yeast, dissolved in ¼ cup water
    1 egg, beaten
    1½ cups milk
    1 teaspoon salt
    3 tablespoons sugar
    1 pound smoked sausage (approximately)
    3½-4 cups flour

Scald milk; cool to lukewarm. Add dissolved yeast and sugar. Add egg, salt and flour to make a soft dough. Let rise. Put one thin layer of dough in a well-greased 9x13x2-inch pan. Cover with sausage; add another layer of dough. Let rise. Bake at 350 degrees for at least one hour, until well-browned.

This is a nourishing supper dish, especially good for fall or winter. Serve with fruit salad and coffee. It really is delicious.

MARIAM H. (PENNER) SCHMIDT '25, faculty

PARSNIP SOUP

    2 pounds pork   8 medium potatoes
    4 medium parsnips   salt and pepper to taste

Cut pork in small pieces. Boil until quite tender, at least 1 hour. Add sliced parsnips, cubed potatoes, salt and pepper. Boil until tender.

LEONA (KOEHN) CLITHERO '43

Waiting for dinner bell at the Boarding Hall - circa 1924

courtesy of **Mariam H. (Penner) Schmidt '25, faculty**

BROWN BREAD

½ cup sifted wheat flour
½ cup graham flour
2 teaspoons shortening, melted
½ teaspoon baking powder
2 eggs
½ cup yellow cornmeal
½ teaspoon salt
1 teaspoon soda
½ cup molasses
2 cups sour milk

Mix dry ingredients. Add milk, eggs, molasses and shortening. Fill can half full. Use tight lid and put into kettle of water. Steam 2 hours.

MAMIE (KENNEDY) PHILLIPS faculty
submitted by LINDA (MUELLER) KAUFMAN '35

Boarding Hall interior - circa 1924

courtesy of **Mariam H. (Penner) Schmidt '25, faculty**

Observations at the Dining Hall Since the Reformation - March 23, 1925

A general atmosphere of order and mannerliness pervades, which is undoubtedly due to the following facts:

The men allow the girls to enter first.

There is perfect quiet while grace is being said (with the exception of an occasional crash in the kitchen).

The waiters have acquired a greater dignity as a result of wearing their white caps.

Eddie Schroeder eats less jam (though this fact is questionable).

Leo Brandt seats the girl who happens to be placed at his left (except when he is too busy teasing the girl at his right).

Nettie Friesen makes brave attempts to check her natural mirth.

Bertha Kaufman never drinks more than six glasses of water.

Jakie Graber tries harder not to be funny.

Bill Penner is not quite so preoccupied. He passes the potatoes after having been asked three times.

Victor Haury does not tease the waiters to give him more milk.

Otto Unruh does not slip fresh onions into the girls' pockets.

August Schmidt drops fewer dishes.

The sweepers stand at attention till diners have left.

Milton Buhler is more dignified than ever.

Sam Kliewer is satisfied with his share of lettuce.

Frieda Becker swipes no cookies.

Elizabeth Dyck, Frieda Enns and Charlotte Regier do not arrive ten minutes ahead of time.

The individuals at the faculty table eat with greater peace and enjoyment.

Graymaroon 1925, page 118

Ted ate so much bread at each meal that a tab was kept on a nearby post. It was not uncommon to see twelve penciled marks for one meal.

Mariam H. (Penner) Schmidt '25, faculty

At chow time, the head waiter would open the double doors and ring a handbell to indicate that the meal was ready. We were all assigned places at the tables, each class seated at a specified table. The faculty had its own table. As we came in, we stood at our places waiting for the waiter to tap the first "ding" on the bell, which meant silent prayer until the second "ding." Or sometimes we would sing the "Doxology." As a country lad, here is where I first learned to eat oysters, and I still like them to this day. I also learned to eat grapefruit.

I milked cows for J. M. Suderman who furnished the dining hall with milk. This meant getting up every morning well before breakfast, so I kept in touch with farm life while attending college.

Louis H. Linscheid '27

Many older Bethel students remember Dr. Doell's broad smile and his flat drawl. One day he conducted our botany class on a tour of the campus to identify trees. As we came to the front of the Administration Building he announced, "And the very last one here is a hackberry." With sly grins, we got into a huddle to discuss the names of the trees before entering them in our notebooks. As we were certain that Dr. Doell's drawl had gotten in the way, we agreed the tree must be a heckberry. Imagine our chagrin when we learned that it was a hackberry. O heck, we really goofed!

Ruth Z. (Dick) Peters '27

Summary school kitchen squad behind the Boarding Hall - 1926

(l-r) _____, Louis H. Linscheid '27, _____, _____, _____, Paul D. Voth '29, _____, Dietrich D. Becker A'24, '27, Elma (Schmidt) Anderson '27

courtesy of **Rosemary (Linscheid) Moyer '52, staff**

CORN SLAW

16-ounce can whole kernel corn, drained
1 small onion, chopped
1 green pepper, chopped
3-4 carrots, chopped
½ cup sour cream
½ cup mayonnaise
¼ cup vinegar
¼ cup sugar
salt and pepper to taste

Combine corn, onion, green pepper and carrots. Combine sour cream, mayonnaise, vinegar, sugar, salt and pepper. Combine vegetables and dressing. Refrigerate at least 2 hours before serving. Makes 6-8 servings.

Note: May substitute 2 cups fresh corn, cut from cob and steamed.

RUTH Z. (DICK) PETERS '27

MAPLE NUT MOLD

3 cups brown sugar
¾ cup cornstarch
3½ cups water

6 egg whites
⅝ cup nuts

Caramelize ⅓ of the sugar. Blend cornstarch and remaining sugar with ½ cup water. Heat remaining 3 cups water; add cornstarch mixture and stir until thick. Cook 20 minutes over hot water. Remove from heat and fold in well-beaten egg whites. Add nuts and pour into wet pans to set. Cut into squares. Serve with soft custard:

1 cup milk
⅜ cup sugar

6 egg yolks
⅜ teaspoon vanilla

Cook as for soft custard. Thin with ½ cup cream.

MAMIE (KENNEDY) PHILLIPS, faculty
submitted by SUE (UNRUH) PACK '37

GOLDENROD EGGS

6 hard-boiled eggs
2 cups medium white sauce
6 slices toast

salt and pepper
paprika

Chop egg whites; combine with white sauce. Season to taste. Heat thoroughly. Pour over buttered toast; pile sieved egg yolks lightly over top. Sprinkle with salt, pepper and paprika.

EDNA (KLIEWER) LINSCHEID x'32

The butter was so strong it stood up to talk to the coffee, but the coffee was too weak to answer.
Mose Stucky '35

Food preparation staff at Boarding Hall entrance - 1928-29

(back l-r) Marie Baergen '37, Buena (Dirks) Voth x'31, Samuel Richert '46, Herman Will x'32

(middle l-r) Menno D. Voth '29, Hazel (Kitch) Bauer '29, Helen K. (Dyck) Ewert '30, Wilma R. (Schmidt) Unruh x'32, Henry N. Harder '30

(front l-r) Anne D. Warkentin A'26, '30, David D. Eitzen '30, Henry Ewert '31, ____, Hilda (Nachtigal) Harms x'32

BLUE MOUNTAIN COFFEE CHIFFON (Jamaican)

1 package unflavored gelatin	4 eggs
3 tablespoons instant coffee	¾ cup superfine sugar
1 cup water	grated coconut
2 cups milk or coffee cream	small chocolate chips
1 teaspoon vanilla	

Dissolve gelatin and instant coffee in water, stirring over low heat. Add milk and vanilla. Set in shallow pan in the freezer about 10 minutes or until it begins to gel. Meanwhile, separate 4 eggs. Beat yolks with sugar in bowl set over pan of boiling water, until thick and creamy. Stir in coffee mixture. Fold in stiffly beaten egg whites. Pour into glass serving bowl. Allow to set in refrigerator. Decorate top with grated coconut and dot with chocolate chips.

LAURA (GOERING) KREHBIEL x'43

CHINESE FRIED RICE

2 cups cooked rice
2-3 tablespoons oleo or oil
1½ cups ham, finely chopped (or pork or shrimp)
1 onion, chopped
½ green pepper
½ cup cooked mushrooms
2 teaspoons soy sauce
2-3 eggs, slightly beaten
1 cup chicken stock (2 bouillon cubes in 1 cup water)

Sauté rice in oleo until evenly browned (5 minutes). Sauté ham, onion, mushrooms and green pepper a few minutes in another pan. Add a little cold water; cook slowly 10 minutes or until tender. Season with soy sauce, and salt if desired. Add beaten eggs to the rice; stir. Add ham mixture. Add chicken stock; bring to a boil. Cook a few minutes; let stand, covered, about 5 minutes until liquid is absorbed. Stir to mix. Serves 6-8.

Note: A cup or more of cooked peas may be added.

MONICA (DIRKS) GROSS '45, staff

TOP-OF-STOVE MEAL

1 pound ground beef
1-2 tablespoons chopped onion
1 can cream of chicken soup
1 can water
1 package fine noodles
1 bay leaf
salt and pepper to taste
1 cup sour cream

Brown ground beef and onion. Add cream of chicken soup, water, noodles, bay leaf, salt and pepper. Cook until noodles are tender. When ready to serve, add sour cream. Serves 5-6.

Tastes like stroganoff!

MARGUERITE I. (GEIGER) FRETZ x'36

BEEF-LIMA SKILLET

½ cup chopped onion
½ cup diced celery
2 tablespoons butter
1 pound ground beef
1½ cups tomatoes, undrained
¼ cup catsup
1½ teaspoons Worcestershire sauce
dash of Tabasco sauce
2 cups cooked lima beans
1 teaspoon salt
⅛ teaspoon pepper

Cook onion and celery in butter until onion is clear. Add meat; cook until well-browned. Add remaining ingredients. Cover and simmer for 15-20 minutes until flavors are blended. Serves 6.

LINDA (MUELLER) KAUFMAN '35

Cooking in dormitory room - circa 1935

Marvin J. Dirks '36

The Bethel College choir trip of 1935—north to Canada, down the west coast to the General Conference in Upland, north again to Salt Lake City and back home through Estes Park—is, by now, a part of the choir members' nostalgic memories. At many of the churches we were given meals and lodging but, between programs and on the road, we ate our meals off the rear endgate of a rehabilitated bus which carried us and our bedding. Many nights we slept under the sky. The meals had to be simple. One two-burner, cantankerous Coleman stove heated water for us to wash our tin pie plates and old silverware from the college dining hall. Our menus consisted of three-p salad, pork and beans, sandwiches, cabbage salad, canned and fresh fruit. This was during the depression days and students had very little spending money. The maroon and gray bus carried a large sign on each side, "Where Good Friends Meet at the Crossroads of the Nation, Bethel College, Kansas."

Linda (Mueller) Kaufman '35

Choir tour breakfast in the state of Washington - summer 1935

Linda (Mueller) Kaufman '35 (far left), wearing the "Boofus Bird," Bethel's athletic symbol, on her jacket, was in charge of meals on the tour. Food was served from the rear of the bus.

THREE-P SALAD

    1 gallon canned peas
    1 jar sweet pickles
    1 package salted peanuts
    mayonnaise

Drain peas. Drain and chop pickles. Combine all ingredients; toss together.

MAMIE (KENNEDY) PHILLIPS faculty
submitted by LINDA (MUELLER) KAUFMAN '35

Choir tour - summer 1935
    Pitching camp at Detroit Lakes, Minnesota

AUNT KATIE'S ICE CREAM

4 eggs, beaten
2 cups white sugar
2 cups heavy cream
½ teaspoon salt
1 tablespoon vanilla

Beat together all ingredients; pour into one-gallon ice cream container. Fill with milk to within 2-3 inches of top. Insert paddles and put on lid. Place container inside freezer bucket; fasten handle, being sure it is tight and moving properly. Chop ice; layer into freezer bucket, sprinkling layers with coarse salt, until filled. Crank until too hard to move crank. Pour off salted water to within 2 inches from top of ice cream container. Wipe off and remove cranking mechanism. Pull out paddle; scrape ice cream into container. Cover with a double piece of waxed paper and replace lid; insert a cork in lid hole. Cover with chopped ice; salt lightly. Let stand until ready to use. *Enjoy!*

KATIE (GOERZ) KREHBIEL Ax'99
submitted by HELEN (PETERS) EPP

HOT FUDGE SAUCE

6 tablespoons oleo
2 cups powdered sugar
½ cup cocoa
1 cup evaporated milk

Melt oleo in saucepan. Add powdered sugar and cocoa; mix well. Add milk gradually, beating until smooth. Bring to a boil over moderate heat; cook, stirring constantly, about 5 minutes or until thick. Serve hot or cold on ice cream or store in refrigerator and reheat over hot water before serving. Makes 2 cups.

DARLENE (DUERKSEN) GOERTZ '72

This is the recipe used by the women of the Bethel College Mennonite Church for all occasions—ice cream festivals to raise money for the college and the church, the songfest which was held in Kidron Park and the various dinners held for students and faculty. The women did the mixing and the men did the cranking. The kids ran around helping with the salting. Every kid found a spoon and when the containers were opened, each got a spoonful of this delicious ice cream. Until the 1930s, the ice cream was cranked at the rear of the Administration Building. Later the cranking was done at the side of the gym. After Memorial Hall was built, it was done at the west side of the hall. This was a time to exchange news, recipes and funny stories.

Helen (Peters) Epp

Making banquet ice cream behind the Boarding Hall - 1935-36

(l-r) _____, Paul Zerger '38, Marden Habegger '38, John O. Schrag '38

"It looks like chocolate pie."
Graymaroon 1936, page 63

Meal preparation at women's co-op in Carnegie Hall basement - 1935-36

(l-r) Myrtle H. (Goering) Unruh '48, staff, Elda Mae (Goering) Waltner x'38, Wilma (Goering) Krehbiel x'38

TUNA OR CHICKEN CASSEROLE

8-ounce can tuna or ½ pound cooked, boned, skinned, diced chicken
10 ounces grated sharp cheddar cheese (reserve 1 cup for topping)
2 cups cubed day-old bread
1 can chicken noodle soup
1 can cream of chicken soup
1 can cream of mushroom soup
¼ cup green onions with tops, finely chopped
1 cup celery, finely chopped
2-ounce jar chopped pimentos
4 eggs, beaten

Mix and pour into 9x9x2-inch pan. Top with 1 cup crushed cornflakes mixed with 1 cup grated cheese. Bake at 350 degrees for 30 minutes. Let set a few minutes before cutting. Serves 9.

For a 9x13x2-inch pan, double ingredients except noodle soup. Serves 15.

MAXINE WILL '40, faculty

CHOCOLATE CREAM PIE

1½ cups sugar	3 cups milk
5 tablespoons cocoa	3 eggs
½ teaspoon salt	1 tablespoon vanilla
2½ tablespoons cornstarch	½ cup oleo
1 tablespoon flour	baked pie shell

Mix dry ingredients in saucepan. Add enough milk to moisten. Add egg yolks; stir well. Add remainder of milk; heat until it boils and thickens, stirring constantly. Remove from heat; add vanilla and oleo. Pour into pie shell.

Meringue: Beat 3 egg whites and ¼ teaspoon cream of tartar until frothy. Add 6 tablespoons sugar gradually; beat until stiff and glossy. Spread on pie. Bake in 400-degree oven until delicately brown.

LINDA (MUELLER) KAUFMAN '35

RAISIN MUFFINS

  2 cups flour
  ½ teaspoon salt
  3 teaspoons baking powder
  2 tablespoons sugar
  1 cup milk
  1 egg, beaten
  3 tablespoons melted shortening
  ½ cup raisins

Sift flour with salt, baking powder and sugar. Mix milk, egg and shortening; add all at once. Stir just until dry ingredients are moistened but not smooth. Stir raisins quickly into batter. The batter will be lumpy. Fill greased muffin pans ⅔ full and bake in 400-degree oven about 25 minutes. Makes 1 dozen muffins.

HILDA (EDIGER) VOTH '35, staff

One of the good things I remember about dining hall food in the 1930s is raisin muffins. They were served on weekends only because many students went home and the group was small. These muffins were light, fluffy and right from the ovens in the kitchen. I do not have that recipe but use one for plain muffins and add raisins to it.

Hilda (Ediger) Voth '35, staff

This was during the depression days of the 1930s. We were allotted one glass of milk per meal. How could one get more than the allotted glass? The milk was brought in from the college barns by students who milked the cows. The milk was poured into kettles which were on the kitchen tables. We who were enrolled in bacteriology made bacterial colony counts of that milk. At mealtime Harold and I reported to fellow students at our table the astronomical number of bacterial colonies on our culture media. Students pushed their glasses of milk to Harold and me!

Dorothea S. Franzen '37

Student workers at the college dairy - 1936

(l-r) Waldo F. Brandt '39, staff, Aaron K. Schmidt x'39, Robert Lee Schmidt '39

SOUR CREAM CHOCOLATE CAKE

2 eggs	⅓ cup cocoa
1 cup sugar	1 teaspoon soda
1 cup sour cream	1 teaspoon vanilla
1 cup flour	¼ teaspoon salt

Beat eggs; add sugar and beat again. Add cream; mix. Add flour, cocoa, vanilla, salt and soda. Beat well. Bake 30 minutes at 350 degrees or until done.

During the depression the administration made facilities available to students to prepare meals in the girls' dorm (Carnegie Hall). We brought milk, cream, eggs and other groceries from home each week. At the end of the week we occasionally had a cup of sour cream left over so we would bake a cake, invite our hallmates and we all would enjoy warm, delicious sour cream chocolate cake.

META (GOERING) JUHNKE x'37

SPANISH RICE

½ pound ground beef
1 onion, chopped
1 tablespoon salt
1 teaspoon chili powder
1 teaspoon black pepper
2 cups tomato juice
3 cups water
2 cups rice

Sauté first 5 ingredients. Add remaining ingredients; bring to a full boil. Reduce heat and simmer until all liquid is absorbed (about 20 minutes).

MARY ANN (GOERING) PREHEIM '42

In 1940-42 we formed a small dining co-operative in the southwest corner of the ground floor of Carnegie Hall (women's dormitory). A group of 20-25 girls did the planning, buying, cooking and cleaning. We ate for approximately one-half of the dining room fee. A favorite dish which appeared on the menu every week or two was Spanish rice. My family likes it too.

Mary Ann (Goering) Preheim '42

Women's co-op in Carnegie Hall basement - circa 1936

(clockwise l-r) Ruth E. (King) Jones '36, _____, _____, Ruth E. (Roth) Voth '38, _____, _____, _____

MACARONI WITH CHEESE

1 quart macaroni pieces
2 tablespoons butter
2 tablespoons flour
½ teaspoon salt
pinch of paprika
½ quart milk
¾ cup shredded cheese
buttered crumbs

Cook macaroni in salted water. Make white sauce of butter, flour, milk and seasonings. Dissolve cheese in sauce. Pour over macaroni; mix slightly. Cover with buttered crumbs; bake.

MAMIE (KENNEDY) PHILLIPS faculty
submitted by LINDA (MUELLER) KAUFMAN '35

Co-operatives: $3.50 per quarter, to be paid by all students who are permitted to board at the co-operative board clubs. . . . A limited number of students is permitted to work in co-operative boarding organizations on the campus, which is considered a student job, the same as work in the regular college kitchen or dining hall.
Bethel College Catalog 1939-40, pages 20 and 25

Memories of water fights, piles of peanut butter sandwiches consumed in the basement and countless good times are all that remain of the 58-year-old Goessel Hall. The wood frame building was the Goessel High School from 1908-36. Bethel College bought it, moved it to the campus, and added a third story.
The Bethel Collegian, March 18, 1966, page 4

The men's dining co-operative in Goessel Hall appointed me as manager in 1936. I bought whatever was inexpensive. Day-old bread was a staple laced with a delicious and nutritious, albeit repetitious, spread made of equal parts of peanut butter and corn syrup. Grapefruit at five cents each was a luxury.
Delbert V. Preheim '37

Men's co-op in Goessel Hall basement - circa 1940

A brief statement about the college farm may be of interest. The college farm, besides providing necessary food for the dining hall, provides work for approximately fourteen boys. During the year we farmed approximately 250 acres. . . . Our dairy at present consists of 25 potential milk cows. We have 9 brood sows and 68 spring pigs, 43 ewes and 32 lambs, and a flock of 200 laying hens. A small beginning has been made with the college garden. We have had a fair crop of potatoes and a very good crop of tomatoes.

Bethel College Bulletin, Report of the President, Fiscal Year 1939-40 - December 1940, page 16

Chicken house on the college farm - early 1940s
   Roy W. Henry '44

CHICKEN CASSEROLE

   2 cups diced cooked chicken
   3 hard-boiled eggs
   1 can water chestnuts or ½ cup diced celery or both
   1 can cream of chicken soup
   1 teaspoon lemon juice
   ½ teaspoon salt
   ½ teaspoon pepper
   potato chips, crushed
   cheddar cheese, if desired

Mix ingredients. Place in casserole; cover with crushed potato chips and cheese. Bake about 30 minutes or till bubbly. Serves 8. *It is yummy.*

JESSIE (BROWN) GAEDDERT '42, faculty

SCALLOPED CHICKEN

    4 cups cubed cooked chicken
    1 quart broth
    4 eggs
    4 cups cracker crumbs
    1 teaspoon salt
    ¼ teaspoon pepper

Mix all ingredients; bake at 350 degrees for 50 minutes in 9x12-inch pan. Serves 10-12.

This was a favorite for Sunday dinners at the dining hall from 1942-50.

LOLA M. HILL faculty

submitted by LOUISE (DUERKSEN) KOEHN '44, faculty

Booster banquet in Memorial Hall dining room - May 7, 1941

This banquet, the first major event in Memorial Hall, was sponsored by the Newton Chamber of Commerce. The speaker was Deane W. Malott, chancellor of the University of Kansas.

When Ella M. Wiebe was dean of women, the girls all received two- or three-page sheets on etiquette. Then we were invited via handwritten notes, in small groups, to her apartment for tea. Proper dress for these occasions in the early 1940s included a black dress and hat, pumps, purse and gloves. We made polite conversation while eating the dainty cookies and sipping tea.

She also gave a tea for senior women. Good manners, including "correct" use of cutlery in the dining hall, were also emphasized.

Monica (Dirks) Gross '45, staff

DELTA TEA

Cook for 5 minutes:

1 quart water   1 cup sugar

Add:

6-ounce can frozen lemonade   1 teaspoon almond extract
1 teaspoon vanilla   2 quarts water

Serve hot or cold. Makes 15-18 six-ounce servings.

ESTHER (RATZLAFF) SCHRAG '38

LEMON SQUARES

2 cups flour   2 cups sugar
1 cup butter or oleo   4 tablespoons flour
½ cup powdered sugar   1 teaspoon baking powder
4 eggs   ½ teaspoon salt
4 tablespoons lemon juice

Melt butter in 9x13-inch baking pan. Mix 2 cups flour and powdered sugar; add to the butter. Stir and press down firmly. Bake for 20 minutes at 350 degrees.

Beat together eggs and lemon juice. Sift together 4 tablespoons flour, sugar, baking powder and salt. Add sifted mixture to eggs and lemon juice. Pour on top of baked crust while it is hot. Bake 25 minutes longer at 350 degrees. Remove from oven; sift powdered sugar over top while cake is hot. Cut into small squares and serve.

MARTHA (QUIRING) WEDEL x'33

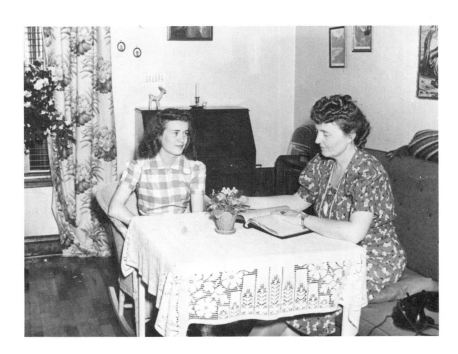

Student conferring with dean of women in her Carnegie Hall apartment - circa 1941

(l-r) Mary Lou (Plumb) Staerkel x'44, Ella M. (Wiebe) Suter x'40, faculty

DINING HALL COFFEE CAKE

    9 eggs
    4½ quarts biscuit mix
    1 teaspoon baking powder
    2¼ cups sugar
    6 cups milk

Spread in greased pan. Sprinkle with crumb topping:

    6 tablespoons cinnamon
    2¼ cups sugar
    1 cup biscuit mix
    1 cup soft butter

Mix thoroughly with fork until crumbly. Bake at 400 degrees for 20-25 minutes. Serve warm. Makes three 12x20-inch cakes.

LOUISE (DUERKSEN) KOEHN '44, faculty
MAXINE WILL '40, faculty
HELEN E. (NEUFELD) JANTZ '54

I ate in the dining room only one year and remember a special kind of coffee cake that was served regularly on Thursdays. On these mornings the early birds often smuggled some to their "lie-abed" friends.

    During my other years at Bethel, I belonged to the women's co-op which met, cooked and dined in the basement of Carnegie Hall. Frugality was the watchword pushed to extremes, one term ending with surplus funds. The following term we didn't hesitate to use up the surplus. The meals that term were superb. There was one particular dish, an orange soufflé, which I was never able to duplicate as deliciously afterwards.

Melva (Goering) Wiebe '47

Honey-topped ice cream was one of the Sunday dinner desserts during the early 1940s. It seems like a simple dessert, yet it was special — like grapenuts for Sunday breakfast, which we still have today.

Selma (Dick) Unruh x'43, staff

Lodging and Board Costs Per Year

Year	Lodging		Board
1893-94	$ 6.00-	10.00	$ 63.00
1900-01	15.00-	29.25	57.60
1910-11	22.00-	30.00	90.00
1920-21	40.00-	50.00	180.00
1930-31	40.00-	60.00	144.00
1940-41	36.00-	60.00	120.00
1950-51		75.00	240.00
1960-61	121.50-	180.00	330.00
1970-71	*303.00-	377.00	495.00
1980-81	**605.00-	705.00	984.00
1985-86	***996.00-	1,210.00	1,396.00

* $40.00 additional for single room
** $302.50 additional for single room
*** $498.00 additional for single room

Information taken from *Bethel College Catalogs*

Students preparing food in Boarding Hall kitchen - 1941-42

    (l-r) Betty (Koehn) Wedel x'45, Gladys (Regier) Vaughn x'44, Elvera K. Voth '46, faculty

Best dessert in college dining hall: a recipe using grapenuts and lemon flavoring.

Monica (Dirks) Gross '45, staff

I remember the head waiter ringing a bell outside the dining hall at mealtime. In five minutes he would lock the front door and no one could get in late. I still remember people pounding on the door, but the relentless head waiter would not let them in.

No one sat in the dining hall until all were at their places. We stood behind our chairs until the head waiter tapped a bell; there was a moment of silent prayer until he tapped it again and we could be seated.

Wednesday was "dress-up" night and the meal was generally a little special. Plates were stacked in front of the table head who dished up each plate and passed it around the table.

Meals I particularly remember are Sunday morning breakfasts with cinnamon toast, grapenuts, and fruit cocktail in a glass cup. Often served at noon in the winter was a combination of sausage, apples and sweet potatoes in one bowl.

Esther P. (Lehrman) Rinner '47, staff

Head waiter preparing to ring dinner bell at Boarding Hall - 1941-42

Elmer J. Buhler '48

GRAPENUT PUDDING

   1 teaspoon lemon rind
   4 tablespoons butter or oleo
   1 cup granulated sugar
   2 egg yolks, well beaten
   ¼ cup lemon juice
   2 tablespoons flour
   4 tablespoons grapenuts
   1 cup milk
   2 egg whites, stiffly beaten

Add lemon rind to butter; cream. Add sugar gradually, blending well after each addition. Add egg yolks and beat thoroughly; add lemon juice. Add flour, grapenuts and milk; mix well. Fold in beaten egg whites. Pour into buttered baking dish and place in pan with 1 inch of hot water. Bake in a slow oven at 325 degrees for 45-60 minutes. Makes 6 servings.

DOROTHY (WEDEL) KAUFMAN '45

PICKLED OKRA

   4 quarts whole okra
   4 heads dill
   4 cloves garlic
   ½ teaspoon alum
   6 cups water
   1½ cups vinegar
   4 tablespoons salt
   2 tablespoons sugar

Place dill and garlic in bottom of each quart jar. Pack okra into jars. Put about ⅛ teaspoon alum per quart on top of okra. Bring water, vinegar, salt and sugar to a boil; pour over okra. Seal. Makes 4 quarts.

LEONA (KOEHN) CLITHERO '43

CHEESE SNACKS

    1 pound cheddar cheese, grated
    ½ cup butter
    2 cups sifted flour
    ¼ teaspoon salt
    ⅛ teaspoon red pepper, as desired

Mix all ingredients to make stiff dough. Divide dough as for a pie and roll between 2 sheets of waxed paper to ¼-inch thickness. Slice into ½-inch strips. Cut into 1-inch pieces. Place pieces on cookie sheet and bake 10-15 minutes at 350 degrees. Store in airtight container.

    Variation: pimento-stuffed olives may be wrapped with the dough. Bake 15 minutes at 400 degrees on ungreased cookie sheet or 20 minutes if they have been frozen.

    These are good served as a party snack or as crackers for soup.

LUCILLE J. (SCHROEDER) LEISY x'39

The college inn was a favorite place to get a snack in the early 1940s since few students had cars to get off campus, and the hamburgers were very good. It seemed quite disastrous when the cost of one doubled in price—from five cents to ten cents!

Monica (Dirks) Gross '45, staff

The college inn is becoming increasingly popular and does a rush business during certain hours of the day. Weather conditions affect the volume and type of business, according to reports. Cold weather increases the demand for hot dogs while a warm spell means a heavy output of ice cream and cold drinks. Three of the girls, Hazel Molzen, Winifred Regier and Venita Krehbiel, are in charge. The enterprise is under the general supervision of Miss Lola M. Hill, dietitian and instructor in home economics.

Bethel College Bulletin, October 15, 1941, page 8

College inn attached to the Boarding Hall - 1941-42

    (l-r) Ruby Ratzlaff x'44, Edwin R. Stucky '42, faculty, Joni "Johnnie" (Kliewer) Bartel x'44

Registration Instructions for Institutional Users of Rationed Foods:

Users of Group I do not receive allotments of rationed foods. They must receive the stamps from the ration books of the persons they serve. Any user may choose to operate on a pooled book basis.

Rationed foods: coffee, sugar and processed foods.

Government Bulletin No.424-10-2-43, February 1943

I remember taking my ration book to Bethel in 1943 for use by the dining hall.

Ethel (Ewert) Abrahams '67

U. S. Office of Price Administration ration book belonging to Ethel (Ewert) Abrahams '67

Sugar Will Be Rationed One Pound Per Person Per Week

Household consumption of sugar will be cut to approximately one pound a week per person under a wartime rationing plan to be placed into effect within a few weeks. . . . There will be enough sugar for each person next year to supply all basic dietary needs, Price Administrator Leon Henderson said in explaining the first rationing of a basic food since the attack on Pearl Harbor. The OPA has already designed rationing books and printing will be started within a few days.

The rationing of sugar arises because the United States imported more than a tenth of its 1941 consumption from the Philippines, because of difficulties of bringing sugar to the U. S. from Hawaii . . . and because of increased demands for making alcohol for use by the army and navy from sugar products.

Mennonite Weekly Review, January 29, 1942, page 1

We converted a lot of recipes from sugar to honey and syrup for dining hall meals. I remember Lola M. Hill spending hours tearing out stamps from students' ration books.

Louise (Duerksen) Koehn '44, faculty

I suggest that those who have enrolled themselves in the course of "Professional Griping" in the phase of dining hall food should go and interview Miss Hill. Perhaps a different slant on the subject could be obtained. No one really knows how difficult it is to plan a menu when you have such a problem as food rationing with which to contend.

The Bethel Collegian, March 1945, page 2

CHILI SOUP

1 cup dry chili beans, cooked
¾-1 pound ground beef
⅓ cup butter or oleo

1 quart tomatoes, drained
salt and pepper to taste
chili powder to taste

Simmer tomatoes 2-3 hours. Heat butter in skillet. Add ground beef; cook until it turns white or browned. Add tomatoes. Add this mixture to beans which have been cooked until tender. Cook mixture slowly about half a day, keeping it below or just at the boiling point. Makes 3 quarts.

MAMIE (KENNEDY) PHILLIPS faculty
submitted by LINDA (MUELLER) KAUFMAN '35

Staff and customers inside college inn next to Boarding Hall - 1941-42

(back l-r) Roland T. Schmidt x'43, Marlon D. Wasemiller x'45

(front l-r) Lawrence Templin '48, Marlo P. Graber x'45, Wilmer E. Goering '50, Winifred E. (Regier) Ewy '43, Venita L. (Krehbiel) Patchim '47

The inn in Memorial Hall basement - circa 1944

(l-r) Bertha Fern (Regier) Gerber x'45, Anne Marie (Regier) Jantz '70, Edgar J. Harder Ax'46, x'52, Donovan Bachman Ax'48, Kathryn M. (Bachman) Penner A'45, x'49, staff, Melvin Boehr '46, Elbert M. Pankratz '48, Elsie A. (Neufeld) Buller '47

Shorts were taboo except on the tennis courts (one wore a skirt over the shorts coming and going) and in gym classes.

Monica (Dirks) Gross '45, staff

Room rent: $12.00-$20.00 per quarter. A fee of $1.00 per quarter will be charged for those with permission to use radios in dormitory rooms.

Board: $40.00 per quarter in college dining hall. Weekly rate is $3.50.

Co-operatives: $3.50 per quarter, to be paid by all students who are permitted to board at the co-operative board clubs.

Bethel College Catalog 1940-41, pages 20-21

The inn in Memorial Hall basement - 1943-44

(l-r) Marie (Funk) Boldt '48, Betty J. (Regier) Wasser '47,

O'HENRY BARS

4 cups oatmeal
½ cup melted butter or oleo
3 teaspoons vanilla
1 cup brown sugar
½ cup dark syrup
¾ cup coconut
miniature marshmallows

Mix first 6 ingredients well. Put in 9x9-inch pan and bake at 375 degrees for 15 minutes or until done. Put marshmallows over crust; bake 2 more minutes.

Frosting:
1 cup chocolate chips
½ cup crunchy peanut butter

Melt peanut butter and chips in double boiler. Spread over baked and cooled crust. Cool; cut into squares. Keep refrigerated.

RUBY (MILLER) KAUFMAN x'42

Sack Lunches

Times will never erase the aromas elicited when thinking of those Sunday evening sack lunches at Bethel. A line would form immediately following Sunday dinner in the cafeteria to receive the supper snack. After all, the sack lunch might be just the right ingredient for a memorable afternoon. A faculty family might invite a group over for a "bring your sack lunch" supper. Friends might drop into one's room at five o'clock to share conversation with the meal. The sack lunch might even be the inspiration for a walk or a picnic in Loewens' pasture.

The sack lunch always included sandwiches—usually ground lunch meat, mixed with a generous amount of mayonnaise and pickle relish (although only the dietitian knew for sure). A second sandwich might boast peanut butter—and, if the budget allowed, perhaps a hint of jelly with it. Relishes consisted of carrots, a celery stick, and the inevitable sweet pickle. There was always a sweet included—a cookie, chocolate cake with peanut butter icing, and perhaps even a fresh fruit if we were lucky. A small package of potato chips usually accompanied this otherwise nutritious meal. But there were always the knowing, telltale signs—the sack had definitely been packed the day before!

Through the years the sack lunch has been the subject of much levity. But who of us would deny the tremendous sociological importance it may have played in creating new and lasting relationships!

Hulda (Gaede) Stucky '45, staff

During the late 1940s, a staff person came to the dining hall to make an announcement following the Sunday noon meal. He preceded his remarks with a sweeping gesture toward the pile of Sunday supper sack lunches where the student waitresses were lined up to hear the announcements. His comment regarding the "bags lined up over there" brought a deluge of laughter which embarrassed the speaker and totally eclipsed the point of the announcement.

Paul G. Jantzen '51, faculty

Eating Sunday evening sack lunches in Carnegie Hall reception room - 1944-45

(l-r) Adeline (Quiring) Friesen '46, Viola (Ewert) Andreas '49, Magdalen (Friesen) Kim '46
courtesy of **Adeline (Quiring) Friesen '46**

Enjoying Sunday evening sack lunches on the bleachers - 1946-47

(l-r) Edna Mae (Boese) Harris '47, Esther P. (Lehrman) Rinner '47, staff

courtesy of **Esther P. (Lehrman) Rinner '47, staff**

In the 1940s dinners were served family style and all students were assigned to a table at which they were to eat for a two-week period. The preferred spot to sit was to the left of the host or hostess at the head of the table, so as to be sure to get some food the first round and not have to wait for the refills. (Some students were notorious for taking overly large helpings so that not everyone would get something.) While there was some grumbling at times over the seating arrangements, one did learn to know many of the students!

Monica (Dirks) Gross '45, staff

I remember some awful-tasting green fruit—the dining hall must have been given gallons and gallons as war surplus or something. Offered frequently as the evening dessert, the sherbet dishes of fruit were simply returned to the refrigerator when we didn't eat any, only to be brought out again. We got smart, accepted the fruit, then salted and peppered it thoroughly to prevent at least those servings from returning ad infinitum.

Anonymous '50

DATE PUDDING

1 cup dates, chopped	1/3 cup melted butter
1 teaspoon soda	1 teaspoon vanilla
1 cup water	1 1/2 cups flour
1 cup sugar	1 teaspoon baking powder
1 egg, beaten	1 cup walnuts, chopped
pinch of salt	

Cook dates, soda and water together until thick. Cool. Beat sugar, egg, salt, butter and vanilla together. Mix in sifted flour and baking powder. Add date mixture and walnuts. Bake in 9x9-inch pan at 350 degrees about 30 minutes. Serve with brown sugar sauce:

1 cup brown sugar	1 cup boiling water
1 tablespoon flour	3/4 teaspoon vanilla
1 1/2 tablespoons butter	

Mix sugar and flour. Stir in water. Cook until thick, stirring constantly. Add butter and vanilla.

Another home economics department favorite from before the days when it was necessary to count calories!

LOLA M. HILL faculty
submitted by WINIFRED E. (REGIER) EWY '43

**Mealtime in Memorial Hall
dining room - spring 1945**

TRIPLE SERVICE RELISH

1 quart carrots, sliced or diced
1 quart string beans, cut
1 quart green lima beans
1 quart sweet corn
1 quart small onions, whole
1 quart cauliflower flowerettes
1 quart small cucumbers
1 pint sweet green peppers
½ tablespoon white mustard seeds *or* pickling spice
4 tablespoons salt
4 cups white sugar
3 cups vinegar

Parboil carrots, beans and cauliflower until tender. Scald corn, onions, cucumbers and peppers. In kettle, combine sugar, salt and vinegar; bring to a full boil. Add vegetables and mustard seeds (or spice); let come to a boil again. Can and seal.

EVA L. (GEIGER) HARSHBARGER x'45, faculty
submitted by HELEN E. (NEUFELD) JANTZ '54

In the spring of 1953, I was in a foods class taught by the home economics instructor, Eva Harshbarger. As one of our assignments, we were to can relish and it was my duty to walk to the grocery store, then at the corner of Highway 15 and 24th Street, to do the shopping.

After canning this relish, we had several pint jars of a beautiful, colorful vegetable relish. It was only after we were completely finished that I realized I was the only one who had not known that I was to be the recipient of these beautiful jars. Since Vern and I were to be married in August, Mrs. Harshbarger had planned this as a very nice and thoughtful gift for me.

Helen E. (Neufeld) Jantz '54

Food preparation in home economics kitchen, Science Hall - circa 1946

(l-r) Eva L. (Geiger) Harshbarger x'45, faculty, ____, ____, Lola Mae (Regier) Friesen '46, ____, ____, ____

*It Wouldn't Be Sunday
Without Zwieback*

*Among the customs of the Low
German Russian Mennonites, the
baking of zwieback has become
almost synonymous with Saturday.
. . . The mother would mix the
large bowlfuls of dough on
Saturday mornings. After several
hours, during which time the
dough was allowed to rise, came
the interesting act of forming the
zwieback. Skillfully the two balls of
dough were pinched from the
large mass in the bowl—one ball,
a tiny bit larger than the other,
formed the bottom of the unique
"roll" into which the smaller ball
was pressed.*

*When finally the zwieback
were in the oven, a most delicious
aroma filled every part of the
house and was wafted outdoors,
luring children in from their play to
beg for the freshly-baked rolls with
golden, crunchy crusts and a
flavor which has hardly been
excelled.*

*Large quantities of zwieback
were made. They appeared first at
Saturday suppers and were again
relished for Sunday breakfasts.
There were always enough for
Sunday suppers, too. . . . Mennonites loved to visit one another
on Sundays. Entire families
spent the afternoon at the grand-
parents' home, with other rela-
tives or friends. The highlight
of the afternoon was always the
serving of vesper. Eagerly all those
present gathered about the long
tables laden with zwieback, jellies,
and perhaps mus and cold cuts.*

*Other occasions which called
for zwieback and coffee as the
medium for fellowship and the
expression of hospitality were
engagement parties, birthday
parties . . . weddings, funerals
and holidays.*

Wilma Toews, '39, faculty, in
Mennonite Life, January 1948,
page 42

ZWIEBACK

    2 cups milk
    ½ cup oleo
    4 tablespoons sugar
    1 tablespoon salt
    2 packages yeast
    8 cups flour

Melt oleo in warm milk. Add sugar, salt and yeast dissolved
in ½ cup warm water. Add flour to make a soft dough.
Knead on floured board until dough is velvety and elastic.
Let rise in warm place until double in size. Punch down and
let rise again until double. Form dough into small balls, placing one on top of the other. Let rise until almost double and
bake at 375 degrees about 10-15 minutes or until golden
brown. Makes about 2 dozen.

WILMA TOEWS '39, faculty

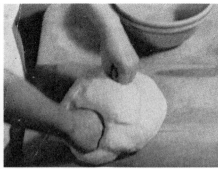

Making zwieback - 1947
Wilma Toews '39, faculty

ELLA'S MACARONI

6-ounce package macaroni
1 tablespoon butter
10½-ounce can condensed tomato soup
½ pound sharp cheddar cheese, grated
1 cup sour cream
6 wieners, cut into ¾-inch pieces
salt and pepper

Cook macaroni in boiling salted water until tender; drain. Add butter, soup and cheese. Cook over low heat until cheese melts, stirring constantly. Stir in sour cream, wieners and seasoning. Heat thoroughly. Serves 6.

A dining hall favorite.

LOUISE (DUERKSEN) KOEHN '44, faculty
MAXINE WILL '40, faculty

Keeping "Post"ed

It may be of some interest to those who eat in the dining hall to know just how their $90.00 a quarter board fee is spent. If this sum is broken down, the daily expenditure for each student is $1.07. Of this amount, 65 percent is spent for food costs. With food costs as high as they are these days, spending 69 cents a day for food is very reasonable. The evening meat serving per person averages from 18-25 cents, so that takes quite a chunk out of the total. Serving roast beef would cost about 30 cents per serving, so one can see why the dietitian omits this meat from the menu. The remaining 35 percent of the fee is used to defray overhead expenses.

The Bethel Collegian, November 16, 1951, page 3

During the late 1940s or early 1950s, Harold Duerksen was in charge of the breakfast coffee urn. One morning a note on the coffee maker pleaded, "Don't make fun of our coffee! You too may be old and weak some day."

Paul G. Jantzen '51, faculty

Food preparation staff in Memorial Hall kitchen - circa 1948

(l-r) Ella Duerksen, Marie (Peters) Peters, Elizabeth (Miller) Roupp, Lena (Pauls) Veendorp, staff, Esther (Pauls) Kaufman x'51

Founders' Day Program

To celebrate the 53rd anniversary of the laying of the cornerstone of Bethel College, there will be a special program in the afternoon. All friends of Bethel are invited. Churches are urged to receive a special offering. The finishing of the Memorial Hall will require funds. Other gifts such as canned fruit and vegetables, potatoes, meat, etc. are needed and will be gratefully received. All are invited to join in making this a big day for Bethel College.

Bethel College Bulletin, October 1, 1941, page 8

Founders' Day banquet in Memorial Hall dining room - October 1948

Faculty members are seated at ends of the tables.

DATE PUDDING

½ - ¾ cup sugar
1½ cups flour
2 teaspoons baking powder
⅛ teaspoon salt
¾ cup milk
1½ cups chopped dates
1 cup chopped nuts
1 teaspoon vanilla
1½ cups water
1 cup brown sugar
2 tablespoons melted butter or oleo

Mix first 8 ingredients; pour into 9x13-inch greased pan. Dissolve brown sugar in hot water. Add oleo and pour over batter. Bake at 350 degrees for 45 minutes. Cool before serving. Serve topped with whipped cream or vanilla ice cream.

This dessert was prepared by the Bethel College Women's Association and served at many of their benefit dinners.

MILDRED H. (HAURY) BRANDT '30
submitted by BARBARA (BRANDT) NEUFELD x'55

PLAIN BLANC MANGE

2⅓ cups milk
⅓ cup cornstarch
⅓ cup cold water
⅓ teaspoon salt
¾ teaspoon vanilla
¼ cup sugar

Heat milk. Mix cornstarch, sugar and salt; dissolve in cold water. Add to milk, stirring until thick and boiling. Add vanilla. Cook. Put into small fruit dishes; add a spoonful of fresh fruit, dates or raisins which have been cooked and thickened slightly.

This recipe was an inexpensive one and used very frequently during the depression.

MAMIE (KENNEDY) PHILLIPS faculty
submitted by LINDA (MUELLER) KAUFMAN '35

The college milk truck makes its round over the campus in the wee hours of the morning while the village is still asleep. It has been observed that the muffler is in need of repair or replacement. The young generation loves the extra noise, but the old folks prefer sleep.

Bethel College Bulletin, October 1, 1941, page 8

Must the Girls Milk?

As was indicated in a chapel announcement recently, there is a desperate need at the college dairy for help with the evening milking, and an appeal was made to girls who know how to milk.

There are no doubt a number of girls among the student body who have been reared on farms who would be glad to don overalls and work shirts and give help in a time of need. In fact, two or three have already responded to the call. However, when this issue presented itself there were some girls who said they would be willing to help with the milking if they felt it was really necessary, but as one expressed herself, "There are too many lazy boys on the campus who kill too much time loafing around."

Before the morning oatmeal has to be eaten without milk or before the cows have to be sold because of the lack of milkers, let's see you members of the "Spit and Whittle Club" don your overalls and work shirts. But, anyway, orchids to the girls who are already on the job!

The Bethel Collegian, February 5, 1943

Feeding time in dairy barn at the college farm - circa 1948-49

(l-r) E. Kenneth Schroeder, staff, Richmond J. Schroeder, farm manager

Milk from the college dairy was available for local residents as well as for student dining - 1951-52

Donald R. Penner x'50

During the late 1930s, Bethel College began a fund-raising event, the Bethel College booster banquet. Tickets were ten dollars a plate. At this rate only the very, very loyal and those who had thrived during the depression could attend. The banquet was held in the old gym (Alumni Hall). I recall the menu included fruit cocktail for appetizer, refrigerator dinner rolls and icebox dessert. In later years, of course, the banquet was moved to Memorial Hall.

Ruth B. (Regier) Geist '38

Women's Association Works for Us

The Bethel College Women's Association, founded in 1934, consists of women from surrounding communities who are interested in Bethel College and its students. The women have done much to improve the equipment Bethel and its students use with money raised by the association.

Through serving banquets and other functions, the women raised enough money to buy floor covering in the dining hall. They have made all the drapes for the basement windows in Memorial Hall. At present, they are working to raise money to build a new girls' dormitory. To date, the association has raised approximately $15,000 of the $50,000 they pledged. The next time you are given a sack lunch because the women's association is serving a banquet, let's remember that they are actually working for us.

The Bethel Collegian, September 27, 1949, page 2

Booster banquet in Memorial Hall dining room - October 12, 1949

(l-r) Edmund G. Kaufman A'09, '16, president, Olga (Reimer) Martens x'39, Hulda (Gaede) Stucky '45, staff, Harry E. Martens '37, faculty

ICEBOX DESSERT

3 cups milk	½ tablespoon vanilla
¾ cup crushed pineapple	⅝ cup nuts
¾-1 cup sugar	¼ cup cornstarch
3 eggs, separated	vanilla wafers

Heat milk and ¼ cup sugar. Blend cornstarch and ½ cup sugar with a little cold milk. Add slightly beaten egg yolks to hot milk; cook until thickened. Remove from heat. Add vanilla. Beat egg whites until frothy; add 2 tablespoons sugar gradually, beating until stiff peaks form. Fold into the hot custard mixture. Place layer of vanilla wafers in bottom of 9x13-inch pan. Sprinkle with nuts and pineapple; add layer of custard. Continue alternating layers with custard on top. Refrigerate. Serve with whipped cream. Makes 12-15 servings.

MAMIE (KENNEDY) PHILLIPS faculty
submitted by RUTH B. (REGIER) GEIST '38

FROSTY STRAWBERRY SQUARES

1 cup flour	½ cup chopped walnuts
¼ cup granulated sugar	½ cup butter

Combine and put ⅔ of crumbs in 9x13-inch pan. Bake at 350 degrees for 20 minutes.

2 egg whites
¾ cup sugar
10 ounces frozen strawberries or 2 cups fresh berries
2 tablespoons lemon juice
1 cup whipping cream or whipped topping

In large mixing bowl, combine egg whites, sugar, berries and lemon juice. Beat at low speed until thickened (about 2 minutes), then beat at high speed until stiff peaks form (10-12 minutes). Fold in whipped cream or whipped topping. Spoon over mixture in pan. Top with remaining crumbs. Freeze 6 hours or overnight. Cut into squares. Garnish with fresh strawberries. Serves 12-15.

MARIE (FRANZ) EWERT x'45

TEA SANDWICHES

Remove crusts from bread. Spread with sweetened condensed milk; dip into chopped nutmeats. Cut into triangles. Heat in 350-degree oven for 5 minutes.

Note: 1 can condensed milk will make 200 sandwiches. There are 30 slices in a pullman loaf.

LOLA M. HILL faculty
submitted by LOUISE (DUERKSEN) KOEHN '44, faculty

Home economics club - 1949-50

(standing l-r) Lorraine E. Galle '50, faculty, Elizabeth R. (Regier) Unruh '51, Josephine (Nikkel) Voth '52, Luella (Zerger) Loganbill '50, Velma Jean (Krehbiel) Balzer '50, Mary Lou (Franz) Duerksen '50, Betty Ann (Enns) Schmidt '51
(sitting (l-r) Wilma Toews '39, faculty, Hope (van der Smissen) Smook '50, Irma L. (Jahnke) Webb '50, Hilda (Schmidt) Unruh '50, LaVerne L. (Linscheid) Boschman '50

"Hen" session in Irish Castle, Carnegie Hall - 1949-50

(l-r) Velma Jean (Krehbiel) Balzer '50, Doris J. (Jost) Heidel x'52, Leora J. (Groening) McFarlane x'52, staff, Lola Fern (Voth) Schmidt '52, Christine (Duerksen) Waltner '51, Mary Lou (Voran) Gaeddert x'52, Marjorie (Linscheid) Isaak '50, Virginia M. (Schroeder) Wiebe '51

COLD WEATHER TAFFY

2½ cups white sugar	1-inch cube paraffin
1½ cups white corn syrup	½ cup sweet milk
1 teaspoon plain gelatin	1 teaspoon vanilla

Soften gelatin in 2 teaspoons water. Set aside. Combine sugar, syrup and milk in saucepan; bring to a boil. Add gelatin and paraffin. Continue cooking to very hard-ball (265 degrees) stage. Add vanilla. Pour into buttered containers; cool. Fold in edges as syrup begins to cool. Repeat until cool enough to handle and pull.

Place a hook on the wall in a cool place. Place candy on hook, pull into a rope, twisting as you pull. Rehook and pull longer each time, up to 12-15 feet. Continue to pull until rope begins to break into threads. Remove from hook, coil on board dusted with powdered sugar. Cut or break into pieces.

Used for taffy pulls at Carnegie Hall.

MAXINE WILL '40, faculty

Food Fests of Irish Castle

Back in the 1940s, most of our dorm feasts (hall feeds) were held Sunday nights when someone returned laden with a generous "care package" of food from home. Word spread quickly. Like vultures, we perched on the hall steps of Irish Castle in Carnegie Hall, the girls' dorm, to devour mackkuchen—that Swiss holiday roll generously filled with home-grown poppy seeds—from Martha Stucky's mother, or sugar cookies and zwieback baked by Ruth (Ewert) Harder's mother. Chocolate cake with fudge icing from Phyllis (Bartel) Regier's mother disappeared in minutes. And Anna Fern (Regier) Lakin dared not return without a generous supply of her mother's light, fluffy cinnamon rolls.

There were meager weekends, however, when we stayed on campus and grumbled about dining hall fare. Dreadfully dull! Horrible! But it was too chilly to brave a cold wind and walk to Newton—few girls had cars in those days—for hamburgers. In desperation we decided Phyllis' corn popper could do more than just pop corn.

"No cooking" was among the list of dorm rules, so it was a challenge to keep our kitchen capers and cooking aromas from the watchful, supervisory eye of Sister Marie Lohrentz. Two dorm delights (low cal, too) prepared in the corn popper were Fire Escape Jello and Saturday Night Soup.

Norma (Jost) Voth x'45

I was too far from home for much home cooking in my Bethel years, so I was truly ready for the great repast of food my roommate, Catherine (Regier) Wiens, brought back to the dorm one Sunday evening. The roast duck, zwieback and other goodies looked and smelled so-o good we decided just once we would not share with other hallmates or whoever had smelled it on the way into "In-du-stray" (name of our hall in Carnegie). So we blocked the door by shoving the dresser in front of it and went to work enjoying every morsel and crumb! Just the two of us.

Meribeth (Nachtigal) Claassen '48

Saturday was the one day of each week when girls were permitted to wear jeans/slacks to meals.

Leola A. Schultz '52

Girls' "Jeans Party"

The student union room was the scene of much activity Wednesday evening, December 7. A strictly informal "jeans party" for all girls was sponsored by the women's dorm council from 9:00 to 10:30. Part of the time was spent in putting up a Christmas tree and other decorations. Recreation consisted of some singing, folk games, and playing checkers, ping pong, dominoes and shuffleboard. Hot cocoa, popcorn and apples were served as refreshments.

The Bethel Collegian, December 15, 1955, page 1

Annual Formal Christmas Banquet

As in previous years, this formal banquet will be sponsored by the faculty. The students are the honored guests. The meal will be prepared and served by the Bethel College Women's Association.

The price will be ten cents for students who regularly eat in the dining hall. Ninety cents will be the charge for faculty and staff members as well as students who do not board at the dining hall.

In purchasing tickets, fellows will be asked for their names and the names of their dates so that the seating arrangement may be worked out. For the girls, either formal or street-length dresses will be in order.

The Bethel Collegian, November 30, 1956, page 1

Every new college administration brings with it changes and new ventures. When Christmas drew near in 1952, we thought an occasion for faculty and staff to get together would be worthwhile. Christmas is always a time for family celebration, but it can include an extended family. We felt the Bethel faculty and staff were such an extended family since all of us were involved in the common task of education. So we began having an annual celebration, inviting the faculty and staff for a Christmas tea at the president's home on Sunday afternoon or evening. Cookies, peppernuts, small rolls, tea and coffee were served during this time of visiting and good fellowship.

Martha (Quiring) Wedel x'33
David C. Wedel A'27, '33, president

Faculty washing dishes after Christmas banquet in Memorial Hall kitchen - December 16, 1953

(l-r) John F. Schmidt '35, faculty, Mildred Beecher x'28, faculty, David C. Wedel A'27, '33, president

BUTTERHORN ROLLS

2 cakes yeast	2 cups warm water
3 eggs	1 tablespoon salt
½ cup sugar	6 cups flour
½ cup shortening	

In mixer bowl, dissolve yeast and 2 tablespoons sugar in 2 tablespoons warm water. Add eggs, sugar, shortening, water, salt and flour. Mix well with mixer. Put dough into greased bowl, cover and place in refrigerator overnight.

The next day, roll to ½-inch thickness in a 12-inch diameter; spread with melted oleo and cut into pie-shaped pieces. Roll from wide edge to the point. Place pointed end down on baking pan. Let rise until double in size. Bake at 375 degrees for 10-12 minutes. Makes 3 dozen.

These were served at all banquets and dinners. Hulda (Penner) Rich made the dough in large quantities in large mixers. The 2 or 3 large dishpans of dough were set in the walk-in refrigerators overnight. The next day 6 to 8 women would come to shape the butterhorns.

LOLA M. HILL faculty
submitted by LOUISE (DUERKSEN) KOEHN '44, faculty

TEA COOKIES

½ cup butter	½ teaspoon soda
¾ cup sugar	½ teaspoon cream of tartar
1 egg yolk	1 cup flour

Knead into small balls the size of a marble. Bake in a slow oven for ½ hour.

MARTHA (QUIRING) WEDEL x'33

HEALTH MUFFINS

2 cups bran buds	2 cups whole wheat flour
2 cups hot water	3 cups unbleached flour
1 cup safflower oil	5 teaspoons soda
¼ cup sugar or honey	1 quart buttermilk
4 eggs, beaten	4 cups all-bran
1 teaspoon salt	

Pour hot water over bran buds; set aside. Using large mixing bowl, mix oil with sugar and eggs. Add flour, salt, soda and bran buds mixture. Add buttermilk and all-bran. Bake in muffin tins 20 minutes at 375 degrees. This batter will keep for 8 weeks in the refrigerator.

EUNICE (UNRUH) ESAU x'50

October 26-28 will be BEAS week at Bethel College. All students, faculty and staff members will want to take note of this grave occasion because BEAS week means Bethel Etiquette At Stake.

During BEAS week a booklet will be given to each student eating in the dining hall. This booklet will show the difference between the Bethelite and the "Graymoron" and should be conducive to forming good table habits as well as correcting deteriorated ones. BEAS week is a project of the foods class.

The Bethel Collegian, October 23, 1953, page 1

Using proper etiquette at breakfast, Memorial Hall dining room - 1953-54

(l-r) Gordon R. Dyck '54, H. Jane (Klassen) Hiebert '54, Florine K. (Voran) Eitzen '56, Donald E. Schrag '56

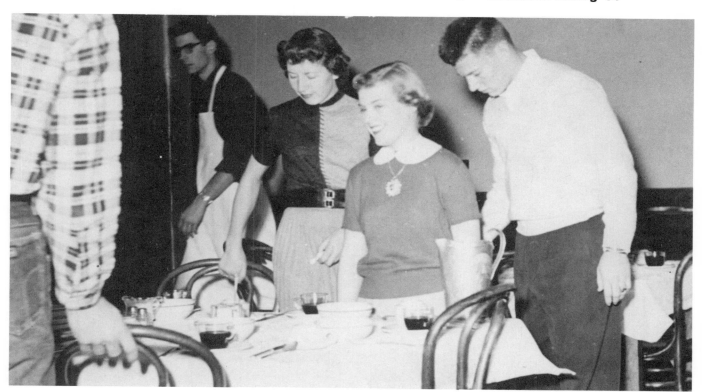

Memorial Hall, completed in 1942, serves as auditorium-gymnasium, dining hall, student union headquarters, college inn, bookstore, classrooms and offices.
Bethel College Catalog 1947-48, page 16

One of the dining hall experiences I remember is trying to eat two whole green gage plums with pits from a sherbet dish. If you tried to cut one with your spoon, the other one would squirt out of the dish. You could try putting the whole plum in your mouth at once, but that seemed uncouth, so the only option left was to leave it uneaten.

Clara (Franz) Reimer '48

VIRGINIA BAKED HAM

1 cup brown sugar	⅛ teaspoon pepper
½ cup hot water	¼ teaspoon powdered
1 cup raisins	cloves (optional)
2 tablespoons vinegar	1 cup currant jelly
1½ teaspoons	(optional)
Worcestershire sauce	cornstarch

Simmer brown sugar and water together 5 minutes. Add remaining ingredients; stir until jelly dissolves. Boil; thicken with a little cornstarch. Pour over baked or boiled ham; heat.

MINNIE (LUND) FRANZ

Stag (male), hen (female) and mixed tables at cafeteria-style noon meal in Memorial Hall dining room - 1954-55

(front table clockwise l-r) Theodore P. Nikkel, Jr. '61, David W. Claassen '59, Kuang-Huan Fan '56, Vernon J. Quiring x'56, LeRoy Klippenstein '56, Loren J. Groening x'57, Abraham Krause '56

Don't always sit with the same group. Have you ever noticed how our dining hall seems to be divided into groups? In the southeast corner you can find mostly Student Volunteer members and student ministers. Here you also find the Leisy Hall table. In the northeast you can find the wheels, while in the northwest abide the barracks bachelors. Finally, in the southwest are found the "chow-hounds" who enter from the south.

Girls, give the fellows a chance to sit near you so they can seat you; and fellows, let our goal be to have each girl seated by some fellow.

Kenneth L. Deckert '53, in *The Bethel Collegian*, February 1, 1952, page 2

"We Believe" . . . What are your comments or criticisms concerning Sunday dinner music in the dining hall?

Excellent—thanks to the generosity of Maynard Janzen who has been transporting his own fine record player to Memorial Hall each Sunday. Good music is appropriate during the once-a-week dress-up occasion in our dining hall. And just consider the element of surprise and variety added to the Sunday fare. Next week it could be Bach, Wagner or even Stravinsky with ham!

Arlo D. Kasper '61, faculty, in *The Bethel Collegian*, December 11, 1959, page 2

In 1953-54 some fifteen to twenty freshman fellows, at the invitation of several upperclassmen, caught a number of sparrows in the hayloft of a barn by blinding them with flashlights.

Returning to the campus, they gained entry to the dining hall through a window. The sparrows were placed under the cups on the tables, which had been set the night before for the family-style breakfast. Toothpicks were used to prop up the inverted cups to give the birds air.

Shortly before the doors were opened, an unknowing waitress noticed a toothpick under a cup and lifted it up. As the first sparrow flew away, she screamed and dropped the dishes she was carrying. The head waiter immediately turned over more cups, releasing more birds. Students entered the dining hall amid flying sparrows. It was discovered that some birds had not survived under the cups.

Word of the practical joke had gotten around the men's dormitory, so attendance was far greater than usual. However, breakfast was served to only the hardy that morning.

Anonymous '60

"Them's Our Sentiments!". . . What Is "shibboleth?"

It is a good term to be used by those people who like to go around to other people asking what a shibboleth is. A good authority on the subject is Miss Will. I think we eat it on Tuesdays and Thursdays.

(Editor's note: see Judges 12:6 for correct answer)

James C. Juhnke '62, faculty, in *The Bethel Collegian*, March 21, 1958, page 2

POTASSIUM PICK-UP

1 cup orange juice
1 ripe banana
2 tablespoons nonfat dry milk
1 cup 2 percent milk
1 tablespoon honey

Mix in blender and serve with ice.

MARTHA (QUIRING) WEDEL x'33

CHEESE BOXES

½ pound grated American cheese
½ pound butter
1 tablespoon cream or milk
pinch of salt
dash of paprika
1 egg white, unbeaten
unsliced bread

Cream butter, cream, salt and paprika. Add egg white and cheese. Cube bread into 1¼-inch cubes; spread on all sides. Heat in 350-degree oven for about 5 minutes or until edges are slightly brown.

Note: the cubes of bread may be spread ahead of time, placed on cookie sheets and refrigerated until time to heat.

LOLA M. HILL faculty
submitted by LOUISE (DUERKSEN) KOEHN '44, faculty

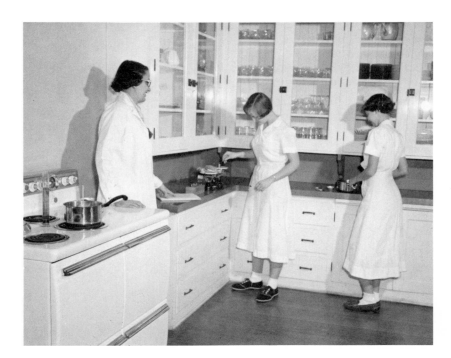

Food preparation in home economics kitchen, Science Hall - circa 1954

(l-r) Virginia (Toews) Stucky x'43, faculty, Luetta E. (Hiebert) Harder x'57, Shirley (Suderman) Goering x'57

SPAGHETTI SAUCE

1 onion, chopped
1/4-1/2 cup diced celery
1 tablespoon minced garlic
1/4-1/2 cup diced bell pepper
11/2-3 pounds ground beef
10 ounces mozzarella cheese
1 tablespoon garlic salt

1 teaspoon oregano
salt and pepper to taste
2 cans tomato sauce
1 can tomato paste
1/2 cup water
1/4 cup sliced olives

Sauté onion, celery, garlic and pepper in a little olive oil. Add ground beef, garlic salt, oregano, salt and pepper. When meat is browned, add tomato sauce, tomato paste, 1/2 cup water and olives. Mix thoroughly. Add grated cheese. Heat gently and stir slowly until cheese melts. Cover and simmer for 2-5 hours, stirring occasionally. Water should cook out and give a thick rich sauce. For thicker sauce, use more cheese; for thinner sauce, use less cheese.

Serve over thin spaghetti which has been cooked in chicken broth or bouillon.

RITA (EWY) EDIGER '74

CROCKPOT SPAGHETTI

1 pound ground beef
1/4 cup chopped onion
11/2 teaspoons salt
1/2 teaspoon garlic powder
1/2 teaspoon dry mustard
1/4 teaspoon mace
1/4 teaspoon pepper

1/4 teaspoon allspice
4 ounces (11/2 cups)
  dry spaghetti, broken
8-ounce can tomato sauce
4-ounce can mushrooms
3 cups tomato juice
1 teaspoon Italian seasoning

Brown ground beef; place in crockpot. Add all remaining ingredients; stir well. Cover and cook on low setting 6-7 hours.

JUDY (FRANZ) DORSING '67

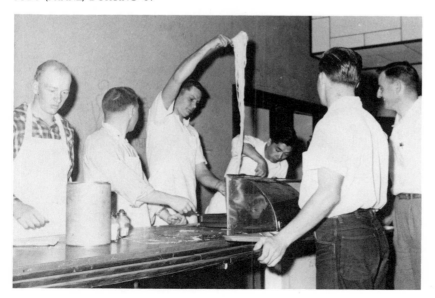

Larry Voth finds his long arm a necessity to escape entanglement while dishing out spaghetti at the junior-sponsored Italian supper last week.

The Bethel Collegian, May 3, 1957, page 3

Serving Italian supper in Memorial Hall dining room - April 1957

(l-r) Allen S. Schmidt '58, faculty, _____, Lawrence Voth '58, faculty, _____, _____, Peter J. Neufeld '57

Sizzling barbecued buffalo meat will constitute the appetizing menu for the semi-annual Bethel College letter club feed, but the shaggy, sturdy young buffalo calf penned in a corral on the Bethel College dairy farm has no suspicion of its fate.

The buffalo calf was on exhibit at the college dairy farm all day Sunday and, providing it does not become too wild at the sight of visitors and try to break out and romp all over the Bethel campus, it will not be shot until the last possible moment, says Clemens Kaufman, president of the Bethel letter club.

The Bethel Collegian, April 29, 1936, front page

The athletic booster banquet tradition, including the popular buffalo barbecues, was initiated in 1935 by longtime Bethel coach, "Otts" Unruh.

Speakers include a wide variety of sports personalities. Selected area high school coaches and athletes are invited as guests of the athletic department. Letter club members sponsor the annual banquet, now open to both men and women.

Bethel College Bulletin, March 1981, page 3

Buffalo barbecue in Memorial Hall dining room - April 29, 1957
Speaker: Don Faurot, football coach and athletic director, University of Missouri

(l-r) J. Winfield Fretz, faculty, Milton M. Goering '50, faculty, Robert J. Standingwater '57, Don Faurot, speaker, John O. Schrag '38, Gerhard Buhr, '50, faculty, David C. Wedel A'27, '33, president

PARKERHOUSE ROLLS

3 cups scalded milk
1 cake yeast, dissolved in lukewarm water
3 tablespoons sugar
4 tablespoons shortening or half butter and half lard
1 tablespoon salt
9 cups flour

Add shortening, sugar, salt and yeast to lukewarm milk. Beat in 4 cups flour and cover. Let rise in warm place. Add 5 cups flour and knead. Let rise until double in size. Roll to ¼-inch thickness. Cut with cookie cutter; brush with butter. Fold in half and press edges together. Let rise until very light. Bake 15 minutes in hot oven.

MAMIE (KENNEDY) PHILLIPS faculty
submitted by LINDA (MUELLER) KAUFMAN '35

DEVIL'S FOOD FLOAT

Mixture I:
> 1 cup flour
> ¼ teaspoon salt
> ¾ cup sugar
> 2 teaspoons baking powder
> 1¼ tablespoons cocoa

Mixture II:
> ½ cup milk
> 1 teaspoon vanilla
> 2 tablespoons melted oleo or butter
> ½ cup nuts, chopped

Sauce:
> 1 cup white sugar
> 2 tablespoons cocoa
> 1 cup hot water

Sift together Mixture I. Mix together Mixture II. Add Mixture I to Mixture II. Put into 9x9-inch greased pan. Cook sauce ingredients for 1 minute and pour over combined mixtures. Bake at 350 degrees for 40 minutes. Serve upside down. Serves 6-8.

This recipe was a favorite with students of the late 1940s and early 1950s. Louise (Duerksen) Koehn was dietitian at that time. It was also a favorite of our family through their years at home.

BARBARA (MILLER) FRIESEN '50

Knights and Knaves of the Kitchen

Clatter! Crash! Rattle! Bang! Three times a day deafening clamor bursts forth from the inner sanctum of the dining hall kitchen as a culinary crew of five faithfully scrapes, washes and dries the hundreds of pieces of silverware and china. . . .

As soon as the dishes are placed on the large galvanized table, the crew snatches them up, whisks off the crumbs, and stacks them in orderly disarray. Another member seizes them from the stacks, flings them into the racks, slides the racks into the eager clutches of the machine, and finally the "Wielders of the Cloth" tenderly and caressingly put the final polish to each piece of ware. After about an hour of such humble but honorable labor, the lustrous china and gleaming silverware is ready to be arrayed in defensive position for another bout with the hungry "Two Hundred."

The Bethel Collegian, March 12, 1943, page 1

Dishwashing in Memorial Hall kitchen - 1957-58

(l-r) _____, Bruce L. Ratzlaff x'61, Donald J. Stucky '67, _____, Samuel E. Schrag '61, Nabil Khabbaz '60, Ingram S. Seah (Samuel I. Hsieh) '59, Harold D. Kroeker '61

LEBKUCHEN

3 teaspoons soda
½ teaspoon nutmeg
½ teaspoon cloves
½ teaspoon allspice
1 teaspoon cinnamon
1 pound dark brown sugar
1 pound walnuts, cracked
   and chopped

1 quart flour
pinch of salt
6 ounces candied fruit,
   chopped
⅓ cup honey
⅓ cup dark syrup
2 eggs

Combine all ingredients. Store in refrigerator for a few days to blend flavors. Put small walnut-sized dabs of dough onto greased cookie sheet; bake at 375 degrees.

HILDA (WIEBE) KRAHN '37

GROGUETTLI (Swiss)

Mix well and quickly:
   4 eggs   2 cups sugar
Add:
   juice of 1 lemon   4 cups flour
   1½ cups ground almonds

Mix well. Roll out to finger thickness and cut into long pieces. Place on buttered pan. Spread egg yolk over top and bake in medium heat.

   This food was used during our MCC service in Switzerland.

ETHEL (SCHINDLER) FAST '59

Reunion of Bethel's Wuppertal exchange students in Wuppertal, Germany - Advent 1958

(l-r) Karin Muehlen '58, Verna (Kaufman) Goering '37, faculty, Rudolf E. Stubenrauch x'56, Janice A. (Waltner) Sevilla '61, Rudolf H. Wiemann '53, Fritz A. Potreck x'55, Anna-Margarete (Voelcker) Gehloff x'55, Harmina (Meerdink) Stubenrauch x'56, Erwin C. Goering '40, faculty, Elisabeth (Friedewald) Rohde x'57

KLEINE ZWIEBACK (Little Zwieback)

2 cups milk
2 cups margarine
1 tablespoon or 1 package dry yeast
½ tablespoon salt
2½ tablespoons sugar
approximately 7-7½ cups unbleached flour

Mix as for any white bread or rolls, kneading in flour until very smooth. Let rise. Roll out on board to ¼-inch thickness, or thinner. Cut shapes with small round cookie cutter (2 inches or less in diameter). Place 2 *cookies*, one on top of the other, on greased cookie sheet. Let rise until double. Bake at 400 degrees until slightly browned (about 10 minutes). Remove from oven. Pull apart to make a single layer of *zwieback*. Rebake at 300 degrees until well-toasted. They will keep well in airtight container, or frozen, if kept out of reach of the family.

To make them extra flaky, save out ¼ of the margarine. Roll dough out on cookie sheet. Dot with margarine. Fold into thirds lengthwise and then crosswise. Let rise again. Roll out as for cutting cookies and proceed as above.

HILDA (WIEBE) KRAHN '37

Faculty and staff coffee break in home economics kitchen, Science Hall - 1958-59

(clockwise l-r) Harold H. Gross '37, faculty, _____, Christine (Oakes) Miller, faculty, Vernon D. Pauls '56, staff, Edmund J. Miller '35, faculty, Ervin H. Schmidt x'36, faculty, Honora E. Becker '24, faculty

We canned approximately 1,300-1,400 gallons of dill pickles for the dining hall over a ten-year period. It was a family project.

Linda (Mueller) Kaufman '35
Peter R. Kaufman '36, faculty

All-school picnic in Kidron Park - 1958-59

DILL PICKLES

3 cups water	cucumbers
¾ cup vinegar	dill
2 tablespoons salt	several cloves of garlic
1 tablespoon sugar	

Combine and heat first 4 ingredients. Pack raw, clean cucumbers into jar. Add dill and garlic. Pour hot liquid over cucumbers; seal. Set jars into warm water; heat over low burner until steaming hot, but not boiling. Remove from heat; let jars rest until they and water are cold.

LINDA (MUELLER) KAUFMAN '35

HOT BURGER SANDWICHES

1½ pounds ground beef	½ teaspoon pepper
1 large onion	1 tablespoon salt
1 tablespoon mustard	1 teaspoon chili powder
2 eggs	2 cups milk
6 crackers, crumbed	

Mix ingredients; bake slowly for 1 hour, stirring occasionally. Spoon mixture into hamburger buns. Makes 20 generous servings.

DINING HALL PICNICS 1942-1950

CHICKEN BORSCHT

3-pound chicken, cut up
1 tablespoon salt
1 teaspoon pepper
3 bay leaves
pinch of ground dill
   or 2 teaspoons dill weed

a few whole peppercorns
2 pounds potatoes, cubed
4 pounds cabbage, cut up
3 cups canned tomatoes
½ pound onions, chopped
1 cup sour cream

Cook first 6 ingredients; cool and place in refrigerator overnight. In the morning, skim off fat, remove skin and bones. Add tomatoes, onion, cabbage and potatoes to chicken broth. Cover with water; cook until tender. Remove spices; add sour cream.

MENNONITE FOLK FESTIVAL - April 5-7, 1962

BEET BORSCHT

ham hock
1 cup dry navy or pinto beans
4 potatoes, cubed
4 cups beets, cut into strips like French fries
½ cup sour cream

Cook beans and ham hock until tender. Add potatoes and beets; cook until done. When ready to serve, stir in sour cream. Serve hot.

MENNONITE FOLK FESTIVAL - April 5-7, 1962
submitted by LINDA (MUELLER) KAUFMAN '35

Serving instructions being given for Mennonite Folk Festival dinner in Memorial Hall dining room - March 11-12, 1960

(l-r) Elma (Goering) Goering, Marie (Krehbiel) Kaufman, Alice (Krehbiel) Kaufman, Linda (Mueller) Kaufman '35, Lorene (Goering) Goering x'39

Ovenkust Attracts Large Crowd of 250

English was taboo in the Bethel College student union room at 6:30 p.m., February 13. Two hundred and fifty people who shared President D. C. Wedel's consternation, "Na jo, wann yie nijh to vael Englisch raede, kaun etj uck waut festoahne (Well then, if you don't talk too much English, I can understand some of it too)," gathered for a Low German supper. Waitresses, dressed in old-fashioned skirts and blouses and crowned with black lace caps that tied neatly under the chin, placed typically Low German foods beside flickering kerosene lamps on the tables. The menu consisted of plumemoos (prune and raisin soup), schinkeflaesch (ham), voarscht (sausage), gebroadne eadshoake (fried potatoes), tweeback (zwieback) and koffee.

Four college girls, Justina Neufeld, Helene Klassen, Marilyn Kliewer and Lois Jahnke discussed schwienschlachte (hog butchering) and kluckesatte (setting a hen) at the faspa (afternoon lunch) table. Others on the program were Mrs. H. R. Schmidt, Betty Warkentine, Ivan Harder, Vera Harder and Joan Banman.

The Bethel Collegian, February 24, 1956, page 4

Frying potatoes in Memorial Hall kitchen for Mennonite Folk Festival - March 11-12, 1960

(l-r) Anna (Bartel) Bartel, Melinda (Wilke) Koppes, Gertrude (Regier) Friesen, staff

BAUERN KARTOFFELN
(Peasant Potatoes)

boiled potatoes
eggs

Boil potatoes with jackets or use leftover cooked potatoes. Peel and slice cold potatoes into lightly oiled hot skillet; brown lightly, turn to brown other side. Break eggs over potatoes, stir slightly; cover for a minute to coagulate egg. Turn onto serving plate. At table, add salt and pepper to taste.

The number of eggs depends on number of potato servings—usually 1-2 eggs per serving.

TENA (FRANZ) SCHELLENBERG '59

SWEET AND SOUR RIBS

2 pounds pork ribs,
  lightly salted
1 teaspoon ground ginger
½ teaspoon garlic salt
¼ cup sugar

¼ teaspoon dry mustard
2 tablespoons soy sauce
2 tablespoons vinegar
1 cup water
2 tablespoons flour

Brown ribs. Add ginger, garlic salt, sugar, dry mustard, soy sauce, vinegar and water. Simmer until meat is done. Add flour to thicken. Serve with cooked rice or fried noodles, or serve with chow mein:

1 can bean sprouts
3 cups diced celery
1 cup diced onion

boiled ham, if available
salt to taste

Cook together until vegetables are crisp-tender.

DOROTHY (SCHMIDT) FRANZ x'44

Mennonite Folk Festival Takes Place on Campus

On March 24 and 25 the Mennonite Folk Festival will once more take place on the Bethel College campus. Following is a tentative schedule of the activities.

From 10:00 to 3:30 there will be a continuous kaffeeklatsch where pastry will be sold for five cents apiece. There will also be weaving, quilting and art exhibitions. The evening meal will be the traditional Low German foods, students eating with the guests. On Friday afternoon and Saturday morning there will be hog butchering at Kidron Kottage.

The Bethel Collegian, March 17, 1961, page 1

Hog butchering at Mennonite Folk Festival - March 24-25, 1961

*Association Provides
Impetus, Inspiration, Income*

*Have you ever thought of peeling
300 pounds of potatoes for one
meal? Or baking 2,500 rolls?
Maybe cooking 250 pounds of
meat? No? Then perhaps you've
never cooked a meal for 1,000
people. The Bethel College
Women's Association has been
doing this on occasions for the
past ten years to complete its
project of raising $50,000 for the
new women's dormitory.*

*Mrs. P. R. Kaufman, in charge
of the social and banquet committee, has one of the biggest jobs
in the association. She must
notify the members when they are
to work and what their jobs will
be.*

*The Bethel Collegian, May 3,
1957, page 3*

**Setting tables for Mennonite
Folk Festival dinner in student
union room, Memorial Hall -
March 24-25, 1961**

**(l-r) Monica (Dirks) Gross
'45, staff, Marguerite I. (Geiger)
Fretz x'36, Mildred (Waltner)
Buhr, Ruby L. (Voth) Stucky,**

OATMEAL COCONUT PIE

¾ cup white syrup
¾ cup coconut
½ cup white sugar
¾ cup oatmeal
¼ cup melted butter or oleo
2 eggs, beaten
1 teaspoon vanilla
pinch of salt
unbaked pie shell

Combine all ingredients. Pour into pie shell. Bake at 350
degrees for 45 minutes.

LOUISE (DUERKSEN) KOEHN '44, faculty

PFLAUMEN-KIELCHEN
(Cold Fruit Soup)

noodles
2 cups unsweetened prunes
2 cups unsweetened apricots
1¼ cups sugar
½ cup syrup
3 tablespoons vinegar
1 tablespoon whole cloves
2 sticks cinnamon

Cook noodles; drain, but save the water. Cook prunes and apricots in separate saucepans, each with enough water to make 1 cupful of juice. Combine cooked fruits. Add sugar, syrup, vinegar, cloves and cinnamon. Add enough noodle water to make a good soup. Thicken it a little.

We had this frequently at home, but it was a "must" for Christmas and Easter. We heated the soup and poured it over cold noodles.

MARIE J. (REGIER) JANZEN A'19, '26

The Bethel College Women's Association recently presented the college with a check for $1,750.54 for an electric meat cutter and two portable warming ovens for the dining hall. Funds were raised by such projects as the German-Swiss foods sold at the Fall Festival and by voluntary dues.

The Bethel Collegian, May 10, 1974, page 5

Mennonite Folk Festival dinner in Memorial Hall dining room - March 24-25, 1961

(servers l-r) Selma (Strauss) Klassen, Phyllis (Funk) Goertzen, Martha (Frey) Schroeder, staff, Marie (Hiebert) Funk, LaWanda (Schmidt) Schroeder, Elda (Bartel) Bartel, Clareen M. (Duerksen) Klassen x'52

DEVIL'S FOOD CAKE

2 cups sugar	½ cup cocoa
½ cup butter	2½ cups flour
2 eggs	1 teaspoon vanilla
1 cup sour milk or buttermilk	1 teaspoon soda

Cream sugar and butter. Add eggs, sour milk, and cocoa which has been dissolved in ½ cup boiling water. Add flour, vanilla, and soda which has been dissolved in a little hot water. Pour into oiled and floured 9x12-inch pan. Bake at 350 degrees for 25-30 minutes or until toothpick comes out clean.

A family favorite. This recipe never fails to make a nice red devil's food cake.

JOANNE (NIKKEL) KLASSEN '72

ROAST BEEF

1-pound roast, cut into 2-inch pieces	1 teaspoon salt
	4 tablespoons catsup
2 tablespoons margarine	⅛ teaspoon pepper
1 medium onion, chopped	2 cups water

Brown meat in margarine in uncovered pressure saucepan. Add onion, catsup, salt, pepper and water. Cover; cook 45-60 minutes. Potatoes and carrots may be added after meat is done; cook 5 minutes longer. *A meal in one.*

AVIS (UNRUH) BRANDT '65

Royalty at "Expect the Unexpected" homecoming banquet in Memorial Hall dining room - November 9, 1963

(l-r) Benjamin J. Stucky '64, LaVerle (Dirks) Schrag '64, Kenneth C. Graber '65, Joycelyn F. (Schmidt) Pool '64, queen, Rosemary J. (Ummel) Hinz '64, Werner Fransen '64

YEAST COFFEE CAKE

1½ cups milk
1 cake yeast
¾ cup sugar
1 egg
½ cup melted margarine
3¾ cups flour
1 teaspoon salt

Warm milk, dissolve yeast and add sugar. Add rest of ingredients and beat until smooth. Let rise until double. Stir and pour into 9x13-inch greased pan. Let rise again. Pour ¼ - ½ cup melted margarine on top and make cuts with knife or depressions. Sprinkle with ½ cup sugar mixed with 1 teaspoon cinnamon. Bake 30 minutes (or a bit longer) at 350 degrees. Serve warm.

I baked this coffee cake many a Sunday afternoon, especially when students were coming for Sunday supper. It is easy to make and always voted "delicious."

ALICE (CLAASSEN) SUDERMAN

Chow in the Sack

A classmate, Glen A. Harder, and I conceived of the project in the fall of 1954. The two of us decided to start a small business. Noting the tendency of students to remain in their dorm rooms rather late on Sunday mornings—well past the usual breakfast hour of the dining hall—it occurred to us that if we delivered breakfast to the rooms we might find many willing to pay for the service. So we tried it. On Saturday afternoons we would go into town and buy frozen orange juice and several types of freshly baked rolls. Early Sunday morning we would mix the juice in gallon jugs and make the rounds of the dorms offering juice and rolls. In the men's dorms we visited each room, pouring juice and offering rolls to students lounging in their beds. Sometimes we would have to find their wallets in trousers hanging somewhere and remove the proper amount of cash so the students would not have to get out of bed! In the women's dorms we simply visited the entry halls, announced our arrival and invited those interested to come down for breakfast.

In fact, quite a few students found the service useful, and we did a pretty good business. We had more fun than profits out of the operation, especially if there were many rolls left over. Any leftover rolls were consumed for Sunday lunch by the two of us! Juice could be left over a week if necessary. Since Glen was head waiter in the dining hall, we used the college kitchen to make the juice. The rolls were stored in our car trunks or back seats.

Robert L. Jungas x'56

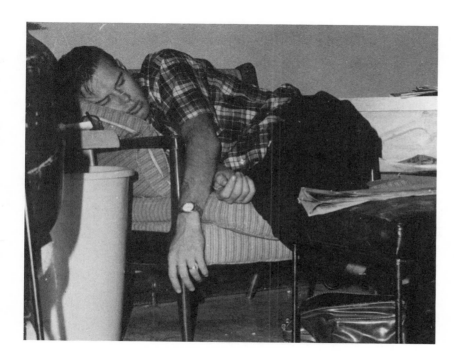

Sleepyhead - 1965-66
John R. Bartel '66

CHOCOLATE CHIP PAN COOKIES

2¼ cups unsifted flour	1 teaspoon vanilla
1 teaspoon baking soda	2 eggs
1 teaspoon salt	12-ounce package (2 cups)
1 cup butter, softened	semi-sweet chocolate
¾ cup sugar	chips
¾ cup firmly packed	1 cup nuts, chopped
brown sugar	

In small bowl, combine flour, baking soda and salt; set aside. In large bowl, combine butter, sugar, brown sugar and vanilla; beat until creamy. Beat in eggs. Gradually add flour mixture; mix well. Stir in chocolate chips and nuts. Spread into greased 10x15x1-inch baking pan. Bake at 375 degrees for 20 minutes. Cool, cut into 2-inch squares. Makes 35 squares.

HOME ECONOMICS CLUB

CLAM CHOWDER

1 can clams	1 can water
1 can water	1 tablespoon butter (or more)
1 can clam chowder	seafood seasoning to taste
1 can water	salt and pepper to taste
1 can evaporated milk	mashed potato flakes

Heat, stirring frequently. Add milk if more liquid is needed. Thicken with mashed potato flakes, starting with 1 cup, and stirring in more as needed.

LUCILLE (FRANZ) HARMS x'53

The inn in Memorial Hall basement - circa 1967

(front table l-r) Howard D. Reimer x'70, Wade Brubacher '70, Margaret J. (Unruh) Stucky x'70, Camille (Gross) Tantibanchachai '70

(back table l-r) Wanda L. (Guhr) Burnett x'70, Michael R. Burnett '69

CHEESE CHARMS

½ cup oleo (room temperature)
¾ cup small-curd cottage cheese (room temperature)
1 cup flour

Combine ingredients; mix well. Divide dough into 3 balls. Wrap each in waxed paper; chill. Roll each ball into a 7-inch circle on well-floured board and cut as for crescent rolls. Roll up, beginning at wide end; place point down on greased cookie sheet. Bake at 350 degrees for 20-25 minutes. Drizzle powdered sugar icing over crescents.

RITA (EWY) EDIGER '74

Students View Issues from "The Other Side"

Bethel's coffeehouse in the old army barracks . . . was created to provide an outlet for creativity and a place where free and open discussion could take place.

A parachute . . . drapes the ceiling, with burlap covering the walls and red-and-blue painted windows completing the basic scheme. Art students donated paintings and drawings. . . . Eight huge cable spools serve as tables with cushions surrounding each spool, and upturned hubcaps hold the cheese-and-cracker companions to coffee. Five kinds of coffee are served from the regular "American" to blends of cinnamon, chocolate, ice cream and cloves.

The Bethel Collegian, April 10, 1968, page 4

An old barrack was converted into a coffeehouse, "The Other Side" - 1967-68

What Is a Frugal Meal?

Ask any Bethel student who ate . . . the evening dining hall meal on February 8 or April 11. . . . The supper menu consisted of a choice of bean or noodle soup, six crackers and a glass of water. The purpose of these two meals was to help defray the expenses of sponsoring a foreign student from Wuppertal to attend Bethel during the coming school year.

The Bethel Collegian, April 20, 1956, page 3

The Bethel College peace club will sponsor a series of "meals of reconciliation" to help provide medical supplies for North and South Vietnam through auspices of the Mennonite Central Committee.

A week-long diet of rice and orange juice accompanied by thoughtful reflection and the knowledge that food money saved will be used for relief work . . . provides a good opportunity for the participants to identify, to a small extent at least, with the Vietnamese people.

The Bethel Collegian, November 3, 1967, page 2

This is the third week of Wednesday fasts at Bethel and, at this point, $1,061 has been raised to support three relief projects. Proceeds have gone to HOPE Enterprises, an Ethiopian relief project; to Jubilee Housing; and to MCC. The food service has agreed to transfer $2.40 for each fasting student into a designated relief project. . . . Response thus far has been exceptional with over 135 students fasting each Wednesday.

The Bethel Collegian, November 18, 1977, page 1

The first fast of this year, October 26, raised $300 which was given to Mennonite Central Committee for its development work in underdeveloped countries. During a fast, be sure to drink plenty of liquids. Water, fruit and vegetable juices, and non-caffeinated drinks such as herbal teas are the best choices.

The Bethel Collegian, November 16, 1983, page 6

LENTIL SOUP

1 cup dried lentils
3 tablespoons chopped onion
½ cup ham, cubed
½ cup peas, cooked
2 cups tomato juice
1½ cups water
¾ teaspoon powdered cumin
dash of garlic powder
salt to taste

Cook lentils until mushy. Cook onions with ham. Combine all ingredients; simmer 10 minutes. Garnish with chopped coriander or parsley leaves.

VERNELLE (SCHROEDER) WALTNER registrar

Rice meal sponsored by the peace club, Memorial Hall dining room - 1967-68

(l-r) Peace Pilgrim, James C. Juhnke '62, faculty

I remember walking back to Goering Hall one night at about 2:00 a.m. after studying, and meeting some deviants in the process of constructing a pyramid of dining hall tables, stretching ten-high. In the dining hall, they set the plates and silverware on the floor in front of the chairs for the breakfast crowd.

Gregory J. Stucky '71

The mysterious character and tradition of "Harvey" is carried on in North Newton by Bethel's own "pooka." His name is Bubbert—Herman Bubbert. . . . This legendary character showed up at Bethel during the 1959-60 school year.

. . . He is best known for his ingenious, prankish character that has added humor and vitality to the college campus.

He would take tests, check out library books and collect bills. He also appeared at the dining hall. In the 1960s students could obtain refunds for missed meals by signing out of the dining hall. Herman would sign out on weekends and then pick up the refund for these meals. This really upset Maxine Will, the dietitian in charge, especially since Herman had never signed in in the first place.

Another incident reported by Herman . . . was the famous case

of the relocated dining room tables. One night forty to fifty students spent two hours stacking the dining room tables ten-high in what was "geometrically a fine construction" in front of the Ad Building. The early breakfast eaters apparently spread the word since "the whole campus woke up and ate breakfast that morning; more people ate breakfast than on any other morning during the year." One might have thought something of this magnitude would be noticed without having to be reported, but Herman nonetheless reported the incident to the proper authorities.

"The Hermeneutics of Herman Bubbert," a manuscript by "The Diggers" oral history group, April 25, 1975

Students were unusually surprised last week by the absence of chairs in the dining hall at breakfast. It was discovered by mid-morning that unidentified persons with excess energy had transported them to a large pile in the Administration Building. Boarders enjoyed the change in routine for several meals until the chairs were returned by various volunteers.

The Bethel Collegian, May 12, 1978, page 1

One of the last memories I have of the old dining hall in the basement of Memorial Hall is the absence of all the chairs one morning! They mysteriously ended up in the dean of students' office. Each student was encouraged by the dean to stop by and get a chair on the way to lunch. However, it was several days before they were all returned to the dining hall.

Anne M. (Herbert) Edwards '80

Dining room furniture relocated at Administration Building - May 8, 1968

courtesy of **Rosemary (Linscheid) Moyer '52, staff**

RICE, GREEN CHILE, CHEESE BAKE

1 cup raw rice, cooked	salt
3 medium zucchini, thinly sliced	2 cups sour cream
7½-ounce can green chiles, chopped	¼ cup chopped green pepper
12 ounces Monterey Jack cheese, grated	¼ cup chopped green onion
	1 teaspoon oregano
	½ teaspoon garlic salt
1 tomato, thinly sliced	2 tablespoons parsley

Butter 3-quart casserole or 9x13x2-inch baking pan. Put in rice, cover with chiles, sprinkle with half of cheese. Arrange zucchini over cheese; add tomato and salt. Combine sour cream, oregano, garlic salt, green pepper and onion; spoon over top. Sprinkle remainder of cheese over all. Bake at 350 degrees for 1 hour. Sprinkle with parsley. Serves 8-10.

HILDA (HAURY) GOERING x'35

SPINACH PROVENCALE

2 pounds fresh spinach	butter
1 large onion, chopped	2 eggs, beaten
1 clove garlic, minced	1 cup Parmesan cheese
olive oil	salt and pepper to taste

Heat enough oil to cover bottom of skillet. Sauté onion and garlic until transparent. Add spinach; cover. When spinach has reduced in size, turn off heat. Add beaten eggs and ½ cup cheese; season with salt and pepper. Pour mixture into buttered 1½-quart baking dish. Sprinkle remaining cheese over top; dot with butter. Bake at 375 degrees for 15 minutes. Serves 4.

NAN (ABRAHAMS) GRABER '71

Noontime cafeteria in Memorial Hall dining room - circa 1970

(l-r) _____, R. Rolan Shilts '73, Robert E. Glick '74, D. Elton Nickel x'74, _____, Sharole (Dyck) Prahl '72

BARBECUED SPARERIBS

several pounds of pork ribs
1 cup catsup
½ cup water
½ cup vinegar
a few drops of liquid smoke
3 tablespoons brown sugar
2 tablespoons Worcestershire sauce
1 teaspoon salt
2 teaspoons mustard

Cut ribs into serving sections; brown in frying pan. Soak ribs overnight in sauce using above ingredients. Bake in 350-degree oven for 1-1½ hours or 4-6 hours in a slow cooker.

DAVID E. ORTMAN '75

FRESH VEGETABLE RELISH

5 tomatoes, peeled and diced
1 green pepper, diced
½ cup celery, diced
1 small onion, diced
1½ teaspoons salt

dash of pepper
2 tablespoons vinegar
2 tablespoons sugar
⅓ cup water

Mix and chill.

DARLENE (DUERKSEN) GOERTZ '72

All-school barbecue in Kidron Park - spring 1972

74

Dining Hall Gets Bright New Look

A new L-shaped counter has been installed. Decorators painted the walls and chairs a three-color combination of bay leaf green, turquoise and celery. The new curtains are turquoise. Another noticeable change is that the wheat and zwieback are gone from the front wall. Instead, pictures of musicians occupy the wall. All meals are served cafeteria style. The mealtimes have been extended to allow time for everyone to be served.

The Bethel Collegian, September 21, 1962, page 2

In 1971 the chairs in the dining hall were painted green, yellow and red; the college inn chairs were painted black.

COUNTRY SAUSAGE CASSEROLE

1-1½ pounds country sausage
4 medium potatoes
4 medium carrots
1 small onion
4 medium apples
3 tablespoons brown sugar

In a 2-quart casserole, layer quartered potatoes, carrot chunks, sausage cut into 1-inch lengths, sliced onion and quartered apples. Top with brown sugar. Add ½ cup water. Cover and bake 1 hour at 350 degrees. Serves 4-5.

A great hit with family and friends.

DENNIS R. KOEHN '75

Mealtime in Memorial Hall dining room - 1972-73

(walking) James L. Voth x'76

(nearest camera) Jane M. (Janzen) Schmidt AA'74

(facing camera l-r) Sherryl R. (Friesen) Lantz x'75, _____, Laura J. (Boehr) Steingard '75, Nancy E. (Voth) Stucky '75, Sharon (Voran) Bergkamp AA'73, Leland A. Dester x'75, Rebecka Stucky '75, Karen F. (Krehbiel) Kaufman '76, Jeanette (Rinner) Grantstein '75

HOT PARTY RYES

12 ounces Swiss cheese, grated
1 pound bacon, crisped and crumbled
      or 5 ounces real bacon bits
4½ ounces chopped black olives
1 grated onion
1 small can mushrooms, chopped fine
dash of Worcestershire sauce
1 cup mayonnaise
4 loaves party rye or pumpernickel bread

Mix all ingredients; spread on bread. Put in single layer, open-face, on cookie sheet; freeze. Place in plastic bags to keep until ready to use. Heat at 350 degrees for 15 minutes. Makes 7-8 dozen.

CAROLYN (MAST) SCHULTZ staff

COFFEE PUNCH

Brew a pot of strong coffee. Spoon 1-2 quarts of vanilla ice cream into punch bowl. Pour hot coffee over ice cream. Sprinkle with cinnamon and nutmeg. Serve.

CAROLYN (MAST) SCHULTZ staff

BANANA TEA BREAD

½ cup margarine
1 cup sugar
2 eggs, unbeaten

3 ripe bananas, mashed
1 cup flour
1 teaspoon soda

Combine margarine and sugar. Add eggs, bananas, flour and soda in order given. Bake in loaf pan at 375 degrees for 25 minutes.

I have served this tea bread many times for coffees and teas, but it is also a favorite with our family. It is simple to make, but delicious.

CAROLYN (MAST) SCHULTZ staff

The 60th, 50th and 25th anniversary classes are invited to the president's home for coffee during alumni weekend - May 1973

(l-r) Lois (Duerksen) Deckert '55, Honora E. Becker '24, faculty

CRANBERRY GELATIN SALAD

1-pound can whole cranberry sauce
3 ounces lemon gelatin
1 cup hot water
¼ cup mayonnaise
1 tablespoon lemon juice
3 ounces cream cheese
¼ teaspoon salt
1 orange, ground
½ cup chopped walnuts

Dissolve gelatin in water. Blend mayonnaise thoroughly with cream cheese. Add to hot gelatin and beat. Add cranberry sauce, lemon juice, orange, nuts and salt. Blend thoroughly with beater. Pour into 1-quart mold. Chill until firm.

VIOLA (FRANZ) BOESE '46

GREEN BEANS

1 tablespoon butter	½ cup sour cream
1 tablespoon flour	2 16-ounce cans beans
¼ teaspoon pepper	1½ cups shredded Swiss cheese
¼ cup milk	½ cup wheat cereal crumbs
1 tablespoon grated onion	2 tablespoons melted butter

Melt butter. Blend flour and pepper; cook until bubbling. Blend in milk; remove from heat; stir in onion and sour cream. Combine sauce with beans and cheese. Turn into greased 1½-quart casserole. Combine crumbs and butter; sprinkle on top. Bake at 400 degrees for 20 minutes. Makes 5-6 servings.

With an all-too-typical dining hall attitude, I remember my least favorite—the okra dishes, rather than the best. This green bean recipe is my substitute suggestion for tasty vegetables.

GLADYS (GRABER) GOERING '40

Christmas banquet in Memorial Hall auditorium - December 6-8, 1973

(facing camera l-r) David H. Suderman '35, faculty, Rosalind (Waltner) Hofer '75, _____, John R. Haury '76

RHUBARB CAKE

5 cups prepared rhubarb
1 cup sugar
3-ounce package
   raspberry gelatin

3 cups miniature
   marshmallows
1 package white cake mix
2 eggs
water

Arrange cut rhubarb in greased 9x13-inch pan. Sprinkle with sugar and gelatin. Top with marshmallows. Prepare cake mix, using eggs and water, as directed on package. Spread batter evenly over marshmallows. Bake at 350 degrees for 55 minutes. Cool 5 minutes. Turn out of pan, upside down, on serving tray. Serve warm. Yields 12-15 servings.

Variations: fresh or frozen thawed huckleberries and lemon gelatin; peach slices and orange gelatin; pie cherries with cherry gelatin (add ¼ teaspoon almond extract to cake mix).

JUDY (FRANZ) DORSING '67

ZUCCHINI PIE

4 cups peeled and sliced
   zucchini
boiling water
½ cup brown sugar
½ teaspoon cinnamon
¼ teaspoon nutmeg

½ cup sugar
¼ teaspoon salt
3 tablespoons flour
3 tablespoons lemon juice
2 tablespoons margarine
pastry for 2-crust pie

Cover zucchini with boiling water; set aside for 5 minutes. Drain; arrange in pastry-lined pie pan. Combine brown sugar, cinnamon, nutmeg, sugar, salt, flour and lemon juice; pour over zucchini. Dot with margarine; cover with top crust. Bake at 350 degrees for 45 minutes.

AGNES (DYCK) JANTZ staff
LELAND JANTZ staff

Dessert reception provided by community Mennonite churches for Bethel family on Goerz Hall lawn - September 1974

(l-r) Nadine Reimer Penner '76, Carol A. Flickinger '75, Vicki (Hinz) Ensz '75, Murray Reimer Penner '75, Frederick M. Loganbill '75, _____, Wayne E. Schrag '75, Galen W. Epp '77

The second printing of Melting Pot of Mennonite Cookery *is available. The Bethel College Women's Association's first 5,000 copies were sold out within five weeks last fall. The cookbook, published last year in honor of the centennial year of the Mennonites coming to the Midwest, includes dishes not only of Mennonite origin. Ten different ethnic groups contributed recipes from their own heritage. A brief history of each group accompanies the recipes.*

Profits from the book go to the women's association for support of projects they undertake for Bethel College. The association recently paid for seven new sewing machines for the home economics department and contributed forty banquet tables for Memorial Hall. The organization also made it possible for the college kitchen to be remodeled at a cost of $5,000. Dr. Edna Kaufman, editor of Melting Pot of Mennonite Cookery, *said the committee found much joy in doing the project.*

The Bethel Collegian, *February 28, 1975, page 4*

February 13, 1983: Bethel College Women's Association members struggled with the decision to print another edition of 5,000 copies of the Melting Pot of Mennonite Cookery. *Only 224 copies remained, with requests for books still being received. Upon the recommendation of the executive committee, the council voted to print a fourth edition, bringing the number of copies printed since 1974 to 20,000.*

Ethel (Ewert) Abrahams '67

Examining new *Melting Pot of Mennonite Cookery*, publication of Bethel College Women's Association - Fall Festival 1974

(l-r) Edna (Ramseyer) Kaufman, faculty, Helen (Peters) Epp, Janet L. (Epp) Van Dyke AA'69

PLEMANIAN SUPPE (Paraguayan Little Pocket Soup)

Cook beef on bones until tender and a rich broth has been formed. Add parsley, bay leaf, peppercorn and salt to beef while cooking. Separate beef from bones and grind. Make dough as for noodles or verenika (flour, salt and eggs). Roll out quite thin and cut into 2-inch squares. Place 1 teaspoon meat on center of square. Fold dough over, making triangles; press around the open side to seal. Place into beef broth with a few sliced carrots and mashed tomatoes. Cook about 15 minutes. Serve and, if you wish, add a bit of cream.

This soup was served to us in 1982 when I was on an MCC tour in Paraguay.

EDNA (RAMSEYER) KAUFMAN faculty

Fall Festival visitors assembling for dinner in Memorial Hall are entertained by swinging games - October 5, 1974

Old-time swinging games entertained visitors waiting for borscht, zwieback and all the rest. Inside Memorial Hall, diners listened to the Schweitzer Ensemble and folksinger Dilores Rempel. Lines moved quickly, with some 1,800 served by the women's association.

Bethel College Bulletin, November 1974, page 2

Bethel College Fall Festival - 1976

Menu No. 1
Sausage

Fried potatoes	Sauerkraut
Rye bread	Zwieback
Cherry moos	Pie
Coffee	Tea

Menu No. 2
Schauble supp (green bean soup)

Crackers	Relishes
Rye bread	Zwieback
Cherry moos	Pie
Coffee	Tea

Menu No. 1 was served in the auditorium upstairs to about 1,200 persons and Menu No. 2 was served in the dining room downstairs to about 600 persons. Adult - $2.50; child under 12 - $1.50; 4 and under - free.

Fall Festival dinner crowd being entertained by folksinger in Memorial Hall auditorium - October 5, 1974

(on stage l-r) Arthur Banman, _____, Dilores F. Rempel '61

On January 23, 1975, WEB Day, LaVonne Platt will give a demonstration of cooking as it might be done in a village of central India. An evening meal featuring foods used in the demonstration will be served in the Bethel College Mennonite Church fellowship hall, prepared by the church dinner committee.

Bethel College Bulletin, December 1974, page 7

Women-Enrolled-at-Bethel (WEB) demonstration of cooking typical of a central India village, Bethel College Mennonite Church fellowship hall - January 23, 1975

(l-r) Kamala J. Platt, '82, LaVonne (Godwin) Platt, faculty

CHICKEN OR BEEF CURRY (Indian)

2½ pounds frying chicken or 2 pounds beef roast

Cut beef into ½-inch cubes; cut larger chicken pieces in half. Remove after browning if using chicken.

Brown meat in ½ cup oleo.

Brown slowly in the same oleo:
  1 large onion, chopped
  ½ teaspoon caraway seeds
  ½ teaspoon whole pepper
  1 large bay leaf, crushed
  ½ teaspoon ground ginger
  ½ teaspoon turmeric
  2 whole cardamom seeds
  ½ teaspoon coriander
  1 garlic clove, chopped
  ½ teaspoon cloves
  2-inch cinnamon stick
  salt

Add 3-4 cups tomatoes or juice; simmer 1 hour. Add 2-3 cubed potatoes and 1-2 tablespoons curry powder. Return chicken to mixture. Cook until meat and potatoes are tender. Water may be added near end of cooking period, also additional salt, if needed.

This may be prepared a day in advance, if desired.

SELMA (DICK) UNRUH x'43, staff

TOMATO JUICE APPETIZER

 1 large can tomato juice
 couple dashes of Worcestershire sauce
 few dashes of concentrated lemon juice
 couple dashes of hot pepper sauce
 teaspoon of sugar
 few shakes of onion salt
 1½ cups water

Shake! Serves 10-12.

MARTHA STUCKY '43, librarian

BARBECUED BRISKET

Sprinkle celery salt, garlic salt and onion salt on brisket. Pour liquid smoke over brisket and marinate overnight. Before putting in oven, sprinkle with salt, pepper and Worcestershire sauce. Bake in foil 4 hours at 275 degrees. Add ½ cup barbecue sauce; bake uncovered 1 more hour. Slice thinly and serve. *Leftovers make very good sandwiches.*

HILDA (HAURY) GOERING x'35

Buffalo barbecue in Memorial Hall auditorium - May 3, 1975
 Speaker: Faye O'Dell, high school coach of Drumright, Oklahoma

 (servers l-r) Michael K. Tieszen '78, Orlin D. Martens '75, Eldon R. Martens AA'75, Jerome Doyle '76, Ronald R. Regier x'78, Glen M. Schmidt '76, Mark D. Christensen '77

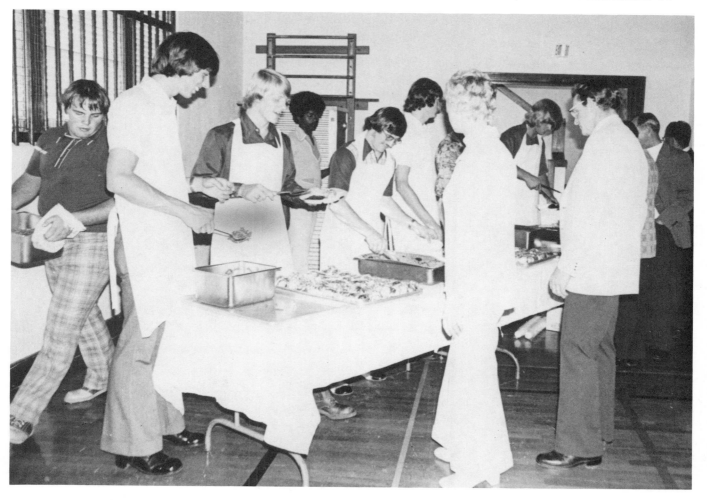

82

When Harold J. Schultz became president of Bethel College, he saw the value of earlier fine arts and folk festivals as a college-community experience. The name of the continuing celebration became Bethel College Fall Festival, often referred to as Fall Fest.

In the first of the new festivals in 1972, the Bethel College Women's Association was asked to have a booth featuring Mennonite traditional baked foods for sale. The committee asked area church women to provide homemade noodles, poppy seed rolls, pfeffernuesse (peppernuts), roggebrot (rye bread) or zwieback to be sold in a booth located between the Administration and Fine Arts buildings. . . . It was so successful that all the food was sold out by noon.

Fall Festival of 1977 listed as responsibilities of BCWA the country store, Kidron Kottage concessions, Voth-Unruh-Fast House open house, bake sale, wheat weaving sales and demonstrations, quilt making, bread and jelly on the green, cookbook sales, cold drinks, auction, demonstration of cookbook recipes, noon meal and the evening barbecue.

Fall Festival continues to be one of the areas of greatest involvement of the women's association and persons of surrounding communities, and one of its chief fund-raisers for the college.

Women of the Hour 1934-84, pages 25, 28, 29

Making pancakes at Fall Festival for benefit of Bethel's soccer club - October 11, 1975

(clockwise l-r) _____, Margie (Peters) Waltner x'79, Ann M. Esau '75, Reanette Boese '76, _____, Rebecca S. (Bergen) Janzen x'79

FOOD PROCESSOR WHOLE WHEAT ROLLS

1/2 cup water
1/2 cup milk
1 teaspoon brown sugar
1 package dry yeast
1 1/2 cups whole wheat flour
1 1/2 cups unbleached flour
2 tablespoons brown sugar
1 tablespoon butter
1/2 teaspoon salt
1 egg

Warm milk and water to 105-115 degrees. Add yeast and brown sugar; let stand 5 minutes or until foamy.

Put flour, sugar, butter and salt in work bowl and combine by turning machine on and off about 6 times. Add yeast mixture and egg; process for 20-30 seconds until dough forms a ball, then process 60 seconds until smooth and moist. Add more flour if necessary.

Let rise until double in size; form into roll shapes. Let rise and bake at 375 degrees.

MARJORIE (HAMON) WARTA faculty

"SCHMECKHAUS" NEW YEAR'S COOKIES

2 tablespoons dry yeast
½ cup warm water
2 cups milk
½ cup sugar
2 teaspoons salt

4 eggs
6-8 cups flour
½ teaspoon baking powder
1 pound raisins, plumped

Dissolve yeast in warm water. Scald milk; add sugar and salt. Beat eggs slightly and add. Mix the above with flour and baking powder. Add raisins coated with part of the flour. Let rise until double. Drop by spoonfuls into deep hot fat. Bake until brown. Yields 50-60.

The flour variation is because some flour is heavier. Dough should be a "hard stir" consistency.

This recipe has been used for a number of years at Fall Festival.

RUBENA (SCHMIDT) FRIESEN

Fall Festival guests purchasing New Year's cookies at the Schmeckhaus - October 6, 1979

Country Store at Fall Festival - October 11, 1975

(clerks l-r) Lois (Sommer) Kreider, Dolores E. (Lehman) Wedel '75, _____, Dolores R. (Flaming) Wiens '65, Carol (Hooper) Stayrook, Lois (Duerksen) Deckert '55

Snack bar in Memorial Hall basement - circa 1975-76

(l-r) Robert E. Stalvey, Jr. x'79, Wendell C. Woolum '76, Harold R. Mack '76, Dale V. Russell '76, Jane E. Friesen '78, _____

KOULOURAKI (Greek Butter Cookies)

3 cups sweet butter
2 cups sugar
6 eggs, beaten
8 cups flour (approximately)
4 teaspoons baking powder
1 teaspoon salt
1 cup light cream
2 teaspoons vanilla
1 egg yolk, beaten
¾ cup sesame seeds (more if desired)

Cream butter until fluffy; gradually beat in sugar. Beat in eggs. Sift together flour, baking powder, salt; stir into egg mixture alternately with cream and vanilla. Knead mixture for 2 minutes. Roll a small ball of dough into 6-inch-long pieces and shape into desired shapes—a braid or a circle. *I often make small round balls.* Brush with egg yolk and sprinkle with sesame seeds. Place on cookie sheets and bake at 350 degrees for about 15-20 minutes. Makes 7 dozen cookies.

DAVID W. KAUFMAN '73

COTTAGE CHEESE APPLE PIE

3 medium apples, peeled and chopped
2 eggs, slightly beaten
1 cup cottage cheese
½ cup sugar
⅔ cup half-and-half
½ teaspoon cinnamon
1 tablespoon lemon juice
pinch of salt
unbaked 9-inch pie shell

Mix ingredients; pour into pie shell. Bake at 375 degrees about 40 minutes.

GLADYS (GRABER) GOERING '40

HONEY WHOLE GRAIN BREAD

3 cups white flour	½ cup honey
2 packages active dry yeast	2 eggs
1½ teaspoons salt	2½ cups whole wheat flour
1 cup water	½ cup regular rolled oats
1 cup cottage cheese	⅔ cup chopped walnuts
4 tablespoons margarine	or pecans
or butter	

In large bowl, combine 2 cups white flour with yeast and salt. Heat water, cottage cheese, margarine and honey until very warm—120-130 degrees. Add warm liquid and eggs to flour mixture. Mix well. Add whole wheat flour, oats and nuts. Add remaining white flour (and a little more if necessary). Knead dough until smooth and elastic. Let rise until double. Punch down and make two 5¼ x 9¼x3-inch loaves. Let rise about an hour. Bake at 350 degrees for 35-40 minutes. Remove from pans onto cooling rack. Top of loaves may be buttered if desired.

This dough is quite sticky, so I spray my hands with a little vegetable cooking spray before shaping the loaves.

A prize winning recipe.

WINIFRED E. (REGIER) EWY '43

PLATZ (Fruit Coffee Cake)

After zwieback have been put on pans to rise, save the last big handful of dough for "platz." Grease a pie pan. Spread dough out thin and bring it up on sides of pan. Brush with melted margarine. Fill with any kind of thickened sweetened canned fruit. If fresh fruit is used, cut into small pieces and coat with sugar. Do not fill plate more than a quarter to half full because the dough will rise and push it out. Bake until done. If the fruit is raw, it should be baked a bit slower than if the fruit is canned.

HILDA (EDIGER) VOTH '35, staff

Customers at Fall Festival bake sale in Memorial Hall lobby - October 2, 1976

Mackkuchen (poppy seed rolls) and zwieback as well as other Low German and Swiss food such as homemade noodles, peppernuts, rye bread and New Year's cookies were sold by the Bethel College Women's Association during the fall fair. Area homemakers contributed their specialties, with the profits going to the association for its project of remodeling Room 213, known as the English literature room, in the Administration Building.

Bethel College Bulletin, November 1972, page 3

Bethel College Fall Festival - 1975

Cabbage borscht, 75 gallons
Beet borscht, 50 gallons
Sausage, 400 pounds
Rye bread, 50 loaves
Zwieback, 90 dozen
Fruit pies, 200
Plumamoos, 50 gallons
Poppy seed rolls, 100
New Year's cookies, 175 dozen

Fall Festival zwieback making demonstration in home economics kitchen, Science Hall - October 2, 1976

(l-r) Marie (Wedel) Banman Ax'26, Clara (Doell) Epp

ZWIEBACK

3 cups skim milk
1 cup safflower oil
1 tablespoon salt
6 tablespoons sugar
2 tablespoons yeast
½ cup warm milk
¼ cup mashed potato buds
9-10 cups unbleached flour

Dissolve yeast, potato buds and 1 tablespoon sugar in ½ cup warm milk. Add 3 cups warm milk, 5 tablespoons sugar, salt and oil. Add flour gradually. Knead for 10 minutes. Let rise until double. Pinch off small balls of dough; place on greased pan. Pinch off a smaller ball of dough and put on top of the other. Let rise 1 hour; bake for 20 minutes at 350 degrees. *This dough also makes good French bread.*

EUNICE (UNRUH) ESAU x'50

WHOLE WHEAT BUNS

3 cups scalded milk
1 cup shortening or margarine
¼ cup honey
¼ cup molasses
3 teaspoons salt
1½ cups cold water
3 tablespoons yeast
6 cups whole wheat flour
5 cups unbleached flour

Scald milk; add honey, molasses, shortening and salt. Mix and add cold water. When lukewarm (120 degrees), add yeast; stir and let sit a minute. Add several cups whole wheat flour; stir. Slowly add remaining flour. Knead 5-10 minutes; place dough in greased bowl. Cover and let rise for 30 minutes. Shape into desired bun size (makes approximately 36). Cover; let rise to double in size. Bake at 350 degrees for 20 minutes. Remove from pans to cool.

This is the recipe which I used to bake the 550 whole wheat buns for the Fall Festival pork barbecue in 1984.

ETHEL (EWERT) ABRAHAMS '67

The evening meal will be a pit barbecue. Beef is to be cooked for twelve hours in a pit to be dug west of Main and 27th streets. A huge bonfire will be started in the pit at 10:30 p.m. on Friday, October 10, with the rest of the food to be prepared and served by the dining hall staff.

The Bethel Collegian, September 19, 1975, page 2

Fall Festival pork barbecue in Kidron Park - October 2, 1976

(servers l-r) Luella (Zerger) Loganbill '50, Varden J. Loganbill '50, Lester G. Ewy x'44, LaVonda (Buller) Claassen

The annual reorganization of the HUB (House Uv Bethel) has been completed. Located in the circular lounge in the basement of Haury Hall, the HUB was designed "to be available as a place on campus for students to eat or get together and as a place to showcase Bethel talents," said Jay Basler, dean of students. . . . During the month of September, ice cream, cookies, and iced tea were sold during the Sunday night films.

The Bethel Collegian, October 12, 1979, page 1

The HUB was created and designed by students and paid for from funds earned on Workday, 1977.

Bethel College Student Guide 1980-81, page 27

"House Uv Bethel" (HUB) coffeehouse in Haury Hall basement - 1976-77

APRICOT BARS

¾ cup margarine
1 cup sugar
2 cups flour
½ teaspoon baking soda
1 teaspoon salt
1 cup coconut
1 can apricot filling

Mix margarine, sugar, flour, baking soda, salt and coconut. Put half of mixture on bottom of greased 9x13-inch pan. Spread with apricot filling and put remaining dry ingredients on top of filling. Bake at 350 degrees for 20-30 minutes.

DAVID E. ORTMAN '75

SNOWBALLS

½ cup oleo
1 cup sugar
2 egg yolks, well-beaten
1 cup crushed pineapple, drained
1 cup nutmeats, chopped fine

2 egg whites, well-beaten
1 pint whipping cream or whipped topping
1 package large vanilla wafers
coconut

For the filling, blend oleo and sugar. Combine egg yolks, pineapple and nutmeats; add to oleo and sugar mixture. Fold in beaten egg whites. Spread filling ½-inch thick on a vanilla wafer; top with another wafer and more filling. Put third wafer on top. Continue spreading wafers until all of the mixture is used. Refrigerate for 24 hours. Two hours before serving, cover each "ball" with whipped cream and sprinkle with coconut to make the "snowball." Chill until serving. Makes 24-30 snowballs.

These delicacies were often made for special dinners served by the women to benefit the college.

MONICA (DIRKS) GROSS '45, staff

CHEESY BAKED PORK CHOPS

Dredge 6 pork chops with a mixture of flour, garlic salt or powder, and pepper. Brown chops in a little oil with chopped green pepper and onions. Place chops in a casserole; cover with cheddar cheese soup mixed with a dash of Tabasco sauce. Bake at 300 degrees until tender, approximately 1 hour.

JOANNE (NIKKEL) KLASSEN '72

Alumni banquet in Memorial Hall auditorium - May 20, 1978

1978 commencement speaker, J. Lawrence Burkholder, president of Goshen College, facing camera in upper left

Lasagna was one of the dining hall's most popular main dishes— at least I never planned to eat out on those pasta nights.

Anne M. (Herbert) Edwards '80

Students, faculty, staff and Life Enrichment participants at Wednesday noon meal in Student Center cafeteria - 1979

(front table l-r) Robert A. Stinchcomb '80, staff, Thomas E. Kiernan '79, Avon A. Degrafenread x'82, Barry L. Carrigan '82

LASAGNA

Step 1:

1 pound ground beef	1½ teaspoons salt
2 teaspoons oregano	1-pound can tomatoes
1 clove garlic, minced	12 ounces tomato paste
1 tablespoon whole basil	4-ounce can mushrooms

Step 2:

2 eggs	1 teaspoon salt
3 cups cottage cheese	½ teaspoon pepper
2 tablespoons parsley	

Step 3:

1 pound mozzarella cheese

Step 4:

10 ounces lasagna noodles

Brown meat; drain off fat. Add remaining ingredients in Step 1. Simmer at least 30 minutes. In bowl, mix ingredients in Step 2. Refrigerate until needed. Slice mozzarella cheese thinly. Cook noodles according to package directions. Layer half the noodles in 9x13x2-inch baking dish; spread with half the cottage cheese filling, half the mozzarella cheese, half the meat sauce. Repeat layers. Bake at 375 degrees about 30 minutes (45 minutes if refrigerated, 1 hour if frozen). Let stand 10 minutes before serving. Serves 8-10.

This can be assembled the day before serving if kept in refrigerator. It may be prepared in two 9-inch square pans— one to serve and one to freeze. *It tastes great reheated!*

ANNE M. (HERBERT) EDWARDS '80

MONSTER COOKIES

1 dozen eggs
4 cups sugar
2 pounds brown sugar
1 pound M & M's
1 pound oleo
8 teaspoons soda
3 pounds peanut butter
18+ cups oatmeal
12 ounces chocolate chips

Bake at 375 degrees for 12 minutes or until light brown.
Makes 7 dozen large cookies.

HOME ECONOMICS CLUB

Home Economics Club Creates Monsters

The home economics club was busy throughout the school year having monthly meetings, baking and selling cookies, and doing local projects. Members baked monster cookies to sell at Fall Fest and for other campus activities. During intermissions at all plays, the club sold doughnuts and drinks. Some of the special projects for the year included taking faculty children trick-or-treating on Halloween, making H.E.L.P. kits for freshmen during first-semester finals week, purchasing club T-shirts, holding a nutrition fair for elementary children, and attending local and state home economics meetings.

Bethel College Thresher 1980, page 57

Home economics club with Cookie Monster on Science Hall stairway - 1979-80

(back l-r, row 1) Lynette M. (Gingerich) Allen '82, Sheree L. (Penner) Leppke '81, Sandra A. Nenfeld '84

(row 2) Julie A. Piel x'82, Rachel K. (Habegger) Pannabecker x'80, staff, Shirley J. (Unruh) Hitt '80, Connie J. (Regier) Kaufman '83

(row 3) Aileen D. (Boese) Esau '81, Tamara F. (Lohrenz) Friesen '82, Sharolyn K. Flaming '82

(front, row 4) Nancy J. Schwartz '80, Mary S. (Unruh) Burkholder '80

The Student Activity Center plays a central part in the daily life of Bethel. It houses such necessities as the dining room, bookstore, snack bar and game room.

The 1982 senior class boasts the distinction of being the first class to use the SAC for four years. The center is one of the few points on campus where both resident and non-resident students regularly congregate for daily meals or merely to stop in for a snack or to get minor essentials at the bookstore.

The Thresher 1982, page 14

Snack bar in Student Center - 1979-80

(l-r) **Keith L. Bartel, '80, Helen R. Scott x'84, Gregory Paul Thiessen, Paul I. Thiessen, faculty, _____, _____, Nancy A. Banman '79, faculty, _____**

HOT JUICY BURGER BUN

1 pound ground beef
½ cup onion (or less)
10½-ounce can chicken gumbo soup
2 tablespoons catsup
2 tablespoons prepared mustard
½ teaspoon salt
½ teaspoon pepper

Brown onion and meat. Add other ingredients. Simmer about 30 minutes. Spoon onto sandwich buns.

ANNA E. (CLAASSEN) LINSCHEID A'13
submitted by ROSEMARY (LINSCHEID) MOYER '52, staff

EASY BIERROCKS

1 pound ground beef
1 cup grated raw potatoes (optional)
½ cup shredded cabbage
¼ cup onion, chopped
½ teaspoon sweet basil
¼ teaspoon allspice
salt and pepper to taste
2 packages crescent dinner rolls

In large skillet, cook together the ground beef, potatoes, cabbage, onion, sweet basil, allspice, salt and pepper until beef is brown and vegetables are done. Drain off fat. Separate each package of 8 rolls into only 4 rectangular shapes; place on ungreased cookie sheet. Pinch together perforations and place ⅛ of the meat mixture on unbaked dough. Fold up sides, sealing edges to keep filling inside. (It makes a neater-looking bierrock when the sealed corners of the dough pocket are placed face down.) Bake at 375 degrees for 10 minutes or until crust is light brown. Serves 8. *Good served with a brown gravy—just like the dining hall served it!*

ANNE M. (HERBERT) EDWARDS '80

Bierrocks were a regular ethnic dish the dining hall frequently served—my first introduction to them! This recipe is made to fit into a fast-paced family schedule. They are great reheated in a microwave oven.

Anne M. (Herbert) Edwards '80

Western Food Service Corporation has already brought some changes to Bethel and more are planned. Some changes already implemented include a switch from artificial to natural flavors in soft drinks, an increased emphasis on fresh-baked breads and some alteration of menus.

The Bethel Collegian, September 1981, page 1

Cafeteria staff in Student Center - 1979-80

(back l-r) Irene Sims, Lydia Zaring, Gene L. Andrews, Emily, Mark Kraner, food service director, Louise (Goertz) Bartel x'49, staff, Loretta Mayberry, Kenneth Evans
(front l-r) Dennis Staley, Kay Soller, Paul Culp

94

CHOCOLATE MARLOWE

40 marshmallows
½ cup milk
6 small chocolate almond candy bars
1 package whipped topping

Heat milk; add marshmallows and candy bars. Let cool. Stir in whipped topping prepared according to directions on package. Pour over graham cracker crust in 9x9-inch pan. Refrigerate.

DOROTHY (HARMS) LOEPP '61

APPLE CRISP (or Fruit Crisp)

1½ cups quick oatmeal   1 cup oleo
1½ cups brown sugar   5 medium apples
1 cup flour

Combine ingredients until crumbly. Slice apples (or other fruit) into 9x13-inch ungreased baking pan. Sprinkle crumb mixture over fruit. Bake 35-40 minutes in 350-degree oven. Decrease sugar if a fruit pie filling is used.
This was a stand-by while our family was growing up.

RUTH (SCHROEDER) KOONTZ '43, staff

Dessert bar in Student Center cafeteria - 1980

Lynda R. (Waltner) Stucky x'82

OVEN CARAMEL CORN

8 quarts popped corn	1 teaspoon salt
1 cup oleo	½ teaspoon baking soda
2 cups brown sugar	1 teaspoon vanilla
½ cup white syrup	

In a large pan, combine all ingredients except popcorn. Bring to a boil, reduce heat and continue boiling for 5 minutes. Remove from heat; stir in baking soda and vanilla. Pour over popped corn. Put in shallow pans, heat in oven for 1 hour at 225 degrees. Remove and cool. Store in airtight containers.

ANNE M. (HERBERT) EDWARDS '80

DILL WEED DIP

1 cup plain yogurt
½ cup mayonnaise
1½ teaspoons dill weed or crushed dill seed
1 teaspoon seasoned salt
1 tablespoon dried minced onion
2 teaspoons parsley

Combine all ingredients. Especially good with celery and cauliflower, also with chips and crackers.

DENNIS R. KOEHN '75

Popcorn: 1. Any of several varieties of corn whose kernels burst open and puff out when subjected to dry heat. 2. An epicurean delight commonly used in residence halls as a medium toward social interaction, boredom relief and insanity control.

Definition from the *Bethel College Student Guide 1980-81*, page 39

Popcorn party in Warkentin Court module - 1980

(l-r) Russ E. Gaeddert '80, Jean M. (Flickinger) Gaeddert '80, Cynthia (Lehman) Linscheid '80, Lisa M. (Habegger) Loganbill '81

BANANA PECAN PIE

1 cup milk	1 teaspoon vanilla
small piece of butter	⅓ cup pecans
1 cup sugar	2 small bananas
2 tablespoons flour	6 tablespoons sugar
3 eggs, separated	baked pie shell

Scald milk with butter. Thicken with sugar, flour and beaten egg yolks. Cook until it thickens; add vanilla. In baked pie shell, place a layer of pecans, sliced bananas and the filling. Top with meringue made by beating egg whites with 6 tablespoons sugar.

VERNA (ROTH) GINGERICH

BEEF BORSCHT

15 pounds stewing beef, cut into 1-inch cubes	dill and parsley
20 pounds cabbage	2 teaspoons pepper
20 pounds potatoes	1 cup salt (or less)
5 gallons water	⅙ cup sugar
3 cups chopped onion or 1 cup dried onion flakes	4 quarts tomatoes
	2 quarts cream

Cook meat 2-3 hours, or pressure cook 45 minutes. Add potatoes a half hour before other vegetables are added. Add cream just before serving (do not boil after cream is added). The stew meat should be well-trimmed; some of the fatty parts may be boiled with the meat and then removed. Serves 155.

This recipe was used at Fall Festival, October 5, 1974.

GLADYS (SCHMIDT) HARMS x'48

Preparing 200 gallons of borscht for Fall Festival noon meal - October 4, 1980

(l-r) Floyd G. Bartel '53, Phyllis A. (Epp) Neufeld '56, Donald R. Penner x'50

SAUCE FOR BARBECUED CHICKEN

3 gallons cider vinegar
1¾ gallons water
8 cups salt
1 ounce paprika
1½ ounces thyme
1 ounce black pepper
1 tablespoon ground garlic
3 cups dried onions
¾ cup Worcestershire sauce

Bring ingredients to a boil. Simmer for about 15 minutes. Strain through a fine cloth to remove particles which may clog sprayer. Add 3 gallons oil. Put chicken on grates 1¼ hours before serving time. Makes enough for 500 halves.

Start briquets 2 hours before serving time.

TABOR MENNONITE CHURCH MEN
submitted by RAYMOND S. SCHMIDT

The chicken barbecue for the Bethel College Fall Festival supper was prepared with anticipation and excitement by the Tabor Mennonite Church men each year for six consecutive years from 1977 to 1982.

The amount of meat barbecued ranged from 1,000 half-chickens in 1977 to 500 quarter-chickens in 1982.

The 1977 chicken barbecue required an above-the-ground pit which was 75 feet long and 4½ feet wide, built by stacking cement blocks two-high.

Raymond S. Schmidt

Barbecuing chicken for Fall Festival in Kidron Park - October 4, 1980

(l-r) Lester L. Voth '64, Bruce K. Schmidt AA'68

98

The first annual Women-Enrolled-at-Bethel (WEB) Day was held on March 26 and 27, 1971. Under the sponsorship of the Bethel College Women's Association, area women were invited to the campus to share concerns, interests and creative plans for developing more effective communications between the college and the community. From this first session, attended by forty women, WEB Day has grown to an attendance of over 300. Half-day courses are designed to offer women the opportunity to pursue a casual or an active interest in a variety of topics such as wheat weaving, wholistic health, quilting, computer awareness, Bible study, solar energy and many more.

Women of the Hour 1934-85, pages 19-22
WEB Day brochures

At Women-Enrolled-at-Bethel (WEB) Day on January 13, some of the record 262 area women attending intently watched a Chinese wok cookery display by well-known culinary enthusiast, Irene King of Wichita. Other classes offered recreational, informative and spiritual enrichment to the participating women.

Bethel College Bulletin, March 1981, page 3

Women-Enrolled-at-Bethel (WEB) wok cooking class in home economics kitchen, Science Hall - January 13, 1981

Irene King, instructor

GREEN PEPPER STEAK

1-pound flank, round or sirloin beef steak, cut against grain in ⅛-inch slices
1 teaspoon soy sauce
1 tablespoon oil
1 teaspoon salt
1 teaspoon cornstarch
pinch of pepper
1 medium onion, diced or sliced
1 teaspoon ginger root (or ⅛ teaspoon ground ginger)
1 teaspoon garlic (or ⅛ teaspoon powdered garlic)
2 tablespoons soy sauce
1 pound tomatoes, each cut into 6-8 wedges
½ cup chicken broth or water
2 tablespoons cornstarch, dissolved in 2 tablespoons water
2 small green peppers, cubed or sliced
1 chopped green onion for garnish (optional)
4 tablespoons oil for frying

Marinate steak for 1 hour or longer in next 5 ingredients. Heat 2 tablespoons oil in wok or skillet until hot. Add onion, garlic and ginger; stir-fry until slightly brown. Add beef and soy sauce; stir-fry until beef is brown. Move beef to the side. Add remaining oil; reheat. Add tomatoes; stir-fry for ½ minute. Add chicken broth; bring to a boil. Stir in cornstarch mixture. When thickened, add green peppers; return beef to the mixture. Continue stir-frying until gravy boils. Garnish with green onion. Serve with hot rice.

WEB DAY CLASS ON WOK COOKERY

STEAK SOUP

1 pound ground beef	½-1 cup flour
1 cup celery, chopped	2 tablespoons beef stock or bouillon
1 cup carrots, chopped	
1 cup onions, chopped	2 tablespoons monosodium glutamate (optional)
2 cups or 10 ounces frozen vegetables (including lima beans)	1 teaspoon pepper
	salt to taste
1-pound can tomatoes	2 quarts water

Sauté beef until red color has disappeared. Sauté celery, carrots and onions in beef drippings or parboil. Run tomatoes through blender with flour. Combine all ingredients and simmer.

This is the soup which was served at the WEB noon meal in Bethel College Mennonite Church fellowship hall for many years.

SELMA (DICK) UNRUH x'43, staff

SPANISH STEW

1½ pounds stewing beef
1 cup tomatoes
½ cup water (or more)
1 small green pepper
1 small onion
salt and pepper to taste
celery salt
chili powder

Dredge meat with flour; brown. Seed and chop pepper; chop onion; strain tomatoes. Place all ingredients into large kettle; bring to boiling point and simmer until meat is done. Before serving, thicken with a little flour mixed with water, stirring frequently. Serves 6.

MAMIE (KENNEDY) PHILLIPS faculty
submitted by LINDA (MUELLER) KAUFMAN '35

During my senior year at Bethel, on Valentine's Day, the dining hall was treated to an incredible "display" of festival spirit by two students who will have to remain unnamed. Attired only in jock-straps and strategically placed hearts, they clutched small bows with rubber-tipped arrows and proceeded through the dinner line, sending heart throbs (and arrows) all around the room. As one diner was heard to remark, "Even as I was telling someone else, I could scarcely believe it myself."

David E. Ortman '75

April Fool's Day prank in Student Center cafeteria - April 1, 1981

Volkswagen owned by Donna M. (Dolen) Stucky '84

In 1979 the home economics club began a project called H.E.L.P. — the Home Economics Lifesaving Program. Sacks of nutritious snack foods, homemade cookies and the like were packaged with a note from the sender, usually parents. Purchased by the concerned parents who wanted to HELP their freshmen through their first week of college finals, they were delivered by home economics club members on Reading Day to the lucky frosh. They sold for $5.00 and, although the home economics club did not make much money on the project, it was continued for several years as a service project to HELP students.

Sheree L. (Penner) Leppke '81

H.E.L.P. Survival Kit - $5.00

Lifesavers, of course
Fresh fruit
Cocoa mix
Memory food - Peanuts (elephants never forget)
Cheese and homemade wheat thins
Sunflower seeds
Sugarless gum
Monster cookies
S'more kit
Druber's wooden coin coupon for late night studying
Panic button

"DAFFY" APPLES

1 cup sugar
½ cup white syrup
15-ounce can sweetened condensed milk
⅛ teaspoon salt
1 teaspoon vanilla

Combine first 4 ingredients in heavy saucepan. Stir well until sugar is completely blended. Cook slowly, stirring constantly to soft-ball stage (it takes quite a while; mixture will be brown and very thick). Remove from heat. Stir in vanilla. While mixture is cooking, wash and dry apples, insert wooden skewers. Immediately after adding vanilla, twirl apples in caramel until well coated. Place on layer of powdered sugar or chopped nuts on waxed paper. Allow to cool.

HOME ECONOMICS CLUB

Assembling H.E.L.P. survival kits in home economics sewing room, Science Hall - 1982

(l-r) Connie J. (Regier) Kaufman '83, Sharolyn K. Flaming '82, Meribeth (Schmidt) Buhr '75

OVEN-BARBECUED MEATBALLS

1½ pounds lean
   ground beef
¾ cup quick oatmeal
1 cup milk
3 tablespoons onion
1½ teaspoons salt
pepper to taste

2 tablespoons
   Worcestershire sauce
2 tablespoons vinegar
¼ teaspoon liquid smoke
2 tablespoons sugar
1 cup catsup

Mix together first 6 ingredients. Form into balls. Place in baking dish; cover with sauce made of remaining ingredients. Bake at 350 degrees for 1½ to 2 hours.

BONNIE R. (FRANZ) EPP '68

OATMEAL SCOTCHIE PAN COOKIE

2 cups unsifted flour
2 teaspoons baking
   powder
1 teaspoon baking soda
1 teaspoon salt
1 cup butter, softened
1½ cups brown sugar

2 eggs
1 tablespoon water
1½ cups quick oats,
   uncooked
12-ounce package (2 cups)
   butterscotch chips
½ teaspoon orange extract

In small bowl, combine flour, baking powder, baking soda and salt; set aside. In large bowl, combine butter, brown sugar, eggs and water; beat until creamy. Gradually add flour mixture. Stir in oats, butterscotch chips and orange extract. Spread into greased 10x15x1-inch baking pan. Bake at 375 degrees for 20-30 minutes.

HOME ECONOMICS CLUB

Beach party in Memorial Hall auditorium - January 1984

(l-r) Thomas B. Shima x'86, Beth A. Harshbarger x'87

Somehow lollipops have become part of Martha Stucky's life. She started making them as a hobby about 1965 while a librarian in Manhattan, Kansas. In 1975 she came to Bethel College to serve as librarian and began selling her lollipops at Fall Festival. She estimates she has made about 12,000 over the years.

Since Martha especially enjoys children's books, many of her lollipops have a storybook character design. These characters include a duck for "Make Way for Ducklings," a horse for "King of the Wind," a cat for "Millions of Cats," a train engine for "The Little Engine That Could" and a monkey for "Curious George."

Each year brings a different use for lollipops and a new challenge for Stucky. In 1984 she made 1,600 candy Christmas ornaments which were used as favors for the Christmas banquet at Bethel.

The Newton Kansan, October 2, 1985

Making lollipops for Fall Festival - September 1985
Martha Stucky '43, librarian

LOLLIPOPS

1 cup sugar	paste color
1/3 cup syrup	oil flavoring
1/4 cup water	

Stir and bring to boil in heavy saucepan. Simmer, covered, for 5 mintues. Uncover and cook until thermometer reads 300 degrees. Do not stir after uncovering. Add a few drops of oil flavoring and color of your choice. Stir to mix before pouring into molds. Add lollipop sticks. Remove immediately when hardened; wrap.

Suggestions without molds: 1) Drip in free-form patties onto cookie sheet or marble slab. 2) Put thin layer in pan and break into pieces when hardened, or put thin layer in gem (muffin) tins. 3) Break into small pieces and add to almond bark for lollipop bark.

MARTHA STUCKY '43, librarian

EVERYDAY VANILLA CARAMELS

1 cup granulated sugar	1 cup milk
1/2 cup brown sugar	1/4 cup butter
1/2 cup light corn syrup	2 teaspoons vanilla
1/2 cup cream	1/2 cup nuts (optional)

Cook all ingredients except vanilla, stirring frequently, to 248 degrees. Add vanilla and nuts. Pour into buttered 9x9-inch pan. When cool, remove from pan, cut into squares and wrap in waxed paper.

LOLA M. HILL faculty
submitted by LOUISE (DUERKSEN) KOEHN '44, faculty

HOT CROSS BUNS

1 cup milk
6 tablespoons sugar
⅓ cup shortening
1 teaspoon salt
2 packages yeast

¼ cup lukewarm water
2 eggs, beaten
5 cups flour
1 teaspoon cinnamon
⅔ cup currants

Scald milk. While hot, add sugar, shortening and salt. Cool to lukewarm. Dissolve yeast in ¼ cup lukewarm water and add to milk mixture. Add eggs, flour, cinnamon and currants. Knead. Let rise until double. Shape into buns. Let rise. When light, mark a cross on each bun with a sharp knife. Bake in 350-degree oven until lightly browned. When cool, frost in crosses with powdered sugar icing.

These hot cross buns are served at the library coffee break each Lenten season. My very-English Grandmother Long always made the first hot cross buns on Ash Wednesday. Frequent baking kept her family supplied with fresh ones during Lenten season. Her daughters followed this custom and so have most of her granddaughters. My family thinks it's an excellent idea. Maybe you will too.

BLANCHE (BROBEIL) SPAULDING faculty

PUMMELCHEN-BERLINERS-BISMARCKS
(New Year's Cookies)

1½ cups milk
½ cup shortening
½ cup sugar
2 teaspoons salt
2 eggs, beaten

1 package yeast
½ cup warm water
1 teaspoon sugar
7 cups flour
oil for deep-fat frying

Dissolve yeast and 1 teaspoon sugar in ½ cup warm water. Scald milk. Remove from heat and add shortening, sugar and salt. Cool.

Gradually add 4 cups flour to milk mixture; stir. Add dissolved yeast and beat; add eggs. Add remaining flour; knead until smooth. Let rise until double. Punch down and let rise again.

Pinch off small portions of dough and press a stewed, sweetened, pitted prune in the center, wrapping dough around to form a ball. Place on lightly floured board and let rise until double.

Drop into hot fat (375 degrees), raised side down, so top will rise while underside fries. Turn, but be careful not to prick them. Drain on absorbent paper.

Roll in granulated sugar while hot, if desired.

Melting Pot of Mennonite Cookery, page 256

submitted by EDNA (RAMSEYER) KAUFMAN faculty

Faculty and staff Thursday morning coffee break in home economics kitchen, Science Hall - fall 1985

(l-r) William Vandever, faculty, Anna (Kreider) Juhnke x'61, faculty, Ira G. Bartel x'44, Mary E. (Roupp) Regier AA'70, staff, Darlene (Diller) Buller, staff, Vickie (Nikkel) Kehr, staff, Edna (Ramseyer) Kaufman, faculty, Christine (Oakes) Miller, faculty, Agnes (Dyck) Jantz, staff

In 1971, our first Christmas at Bethel College, we invited the faculty, administrators, and their spouses to our home for a holiday buffet. The tradition has continued and grown to include the entire Bethel family—faculty and all staff personnel, board of directors, Newton advisory board and spouses. Since the celebration has grown to 300 people each year, every room in the house is used. We decorate the entire house and serve the buffet throughout the evening. It is our Christmas gift to the Bethel family.

Carolyn (Mast) Schultz, staff
Harold J. Schultz, president

Christmas buffet in president's home - December 15, 1985

(l-r) Carolyn (Mast) Schultz, staff, Lucille J. (Schroeder) Leisy x'39, Waldo W. Leisy x'39

HOLIDAY FLORENTINE CREPES

10-ounce box frozen spinach, chopped
1/2 teaspoon salt
1/8 teaspoon pepper
1/3 cup light cream
1/2 teaspoon oregano
1 tablespoon minced onion
1 1/2 cups ricotta cheese
1 cup Monterey Jack cheese, grated
3/4 cup pepperoni, sliced and chopped
1/4 cup grated Parmesan cheese
parsley flakes

Cook the spinach, drain and squeeze dry. Add next 8 ingredients and mix. Fill crepes with mixture. Roll up and place in baking pan; brush with butter. Sprinkle with Parmesan cheese and parsley flakes. Bake at 350 degrees for 15-20 minutes. Makes 18-20 crepes.

An original recipe adapted from crepes Florentine. I served these in quantity (400) for the faculty-staff Christmas buffet in our home. It is a recipe which can be increased or decreased with good results. I would suggest the crepe recipe in Melting Pot of Mennonite Cookery, *page 283.*

CAROLYN (MAST) SCHULTZ staff

ADDITIONAL RECIPES AND ANECDOTES

SHRIMP APPETIZER

8 ounces cream cheese
½ cup oleo
1 tablespoon Worcestershire sauce
12 ounces frozen shrimp, cooked and cooled
2 tablespoons lemon juice
2 tablespoons chopped onions
3 tablespoons mayonnaise

Whip all together. Serve on thin slices of wheat bread.

MARGUERITE I. (GEIGER) FRETZ x'36

DANISH CHEESE SPREAD

9 ounces Gouda cheese, grated
¾ cup crumbled blue cheese (about 3 ounces)
½ cup dairy sour cream
4 tablespoons butter or margarine
2 tablespoons cider vinegar
1 tablespoon grated onion
⅛ teaspoon garlic salt
⅛ teaspoon cayenne pepper

Combine all ingredients in medium-sized saucepan. Cook slowly, stirring constantly, for 15 minutes or until cheeses are completely melted and mixture is blended. Pour into 3-cup crock. Chill at least 8 hours or until firm.
    Keeps well if refrigerated. Best served at room temperature with variety of crackers.

LUCILLE (FRANZ) HARMS x'53

CHEESE-STUFFED MUSHROOMS

1½ pounds fresh mushrooms
8 ounces cream cheese, softened
dash of salt
dash of ground nutmeg
freshly ground black pepper
1 cup grated Parmesan cheese

Rinse mushrooms and pat dry. Remove stems. Place caps on baking sheet. Combine remaining ingredients except 2 tablespoons Parmesan cheese. Mix well. Spoon mixture into mushroom caps. Sprinkle each with reserved cheese. Bake at 350 degrees for 20 minutes. They may be reheated briefly in microwave oven. Yields 4 dozen.

MARTHA A. (PENNER) UNRUH '37

SALMON PARTY LOG

1 pound canned sockeye salmon
8 ounces softened cream cheese
1 tablespoon lemon juice
2 teaspoons grated onion
1 teaspoon horseradish
¼ teaspoon salt
1 teaspoon liquid smoke
½ cup pecans
2 tablespoons chopped parsley

Drain salmon. Mix first 7 ingredients. Divide into 2 parts and make 2 logs. Chill. Spread nuts and parsley onto waxed paper. Roll logs in nuts. Chill several hours before serving.

FRANCES (REGIER) HORAN '38

CAROB FRUIT FUDGE

½ cup honey
1 cup peanut butter
¾ cup carob powder
1 cup sesame seeds
½ cup shredded coconut
½ cup combination of chopped dried apples, apricots or dates

Heat honey and peanut butter in saucepan. Quickly stir in carob powder and remove pan from heat. Add remaining ingredients and turn into lightly oiled 9-inch square dish. Refrigerate to harden. Cut into squares and serve.
    Carob fudge is a terrific treat for the individuals who are allergic to chocolate!

ADELLA (NIKKEL) HARMON '57

BOSTON CREAM FUDGE

6 cups white sugar
2 cups dark syrup
3 cups cream or half-and-half
3 pounds English walnuts or pecans (may use 2 cups nuts)
flavoring, as desired

Mix and boil sugar, syrup and cream, stirring constantly until dissolved, then occasionally. Do not let it scorch. Boil to 238 degrees. Remove from heat, set aside to cool to room temperature. Add nuts and flavoring; beat until no longer glossy. Pour into buttered container and cut into squares. This will keep in a tight container for 4-6 weeks.

MAXINE WILL '40, faculty

ORIENTAL CREMES

2½ cups sugar
1 cup water
1⅓ tablespoons white syrup
⅓ teaspoon glycerin
5 drops acetic acid
1 egg white

In kettle, heat sugar, water and syrup, stirring until dissolved. Add glycerin and continue to heat. When it begins to boil, wipe down sides of kettle with a piece of cheesecloth wrapped on a fork (keep cheesecloth in cold water when not in use). Cook 5 minutes. Add acetic acid, cover and cook 5-10 minutes. Remove cover, wipe down kettle with wet cloth. Boil to 235 degrees. Rinse a platter with cold water; shake. Holding utensil close to platter, pour creme mixture onto platter; do not scrape pan. Set carefully to cool at room temperature. Leave unmoved until thoroughly cold, about 45 minutes. (This is a very sensitive mixture which is apt to become sugary if moved during cooling.) Beat egg white until stiff but not dry, put on top of cooled mixture. Beat with table fork until it will stand alone (20-60 minutes). If too hard, knead in a thumbprintful of water. Divide into quarters or thirds, tint and flavor each part; mold into desired shapes to dip. (These must be put on waxed paper and allowed to dry until the following day.)

MAMIE (KENNEDY) PHILLIPS faculty
submitted by RUTH B. (REGIER) GEIST '38

CHOCOLATE COATING

Buy dipping chocolate at a candy kitchen or grocery store. Shave it into slivers. Place in top of double boiler, suspended over 110-120-degree water. Do not heat. Allow to melt slowly while stirring. Beat with spoon until almost cold. With forefingers, push an oriental creme center upside down into coating. Remove and, with thumb, ease coating to cover bottom of the creme. Clean off underside of forefingers on edge of coating utensil, turn hand over and place the chocolate, bottom side down, on waxed paper. With coating remaining on inside of forefingers, put a soft swirl on top of each chocolate. Cool.

MAMIE (KENNEDY) PHILLIPS faculty
submitted by RUTH B. (REGIER) GEIST '38

The hand-dipped chocolates recipe is most challenging, but so tasty. Mrs. Phillips brought this recipe along with others from Columbia University where she earned her master's degree. This particular recipe is unique in that the centers are oriental cremes, the type used in the most expensive chocolates of the day.

RUTH B. (REGIER) GEIST '38

TOMATO SOUP CAKE

½ cup shortening
1 cup sugar
1 cup tomato soup
1 teaspoon soda
2 cups flour
2 teaspoons baking powder
1 teaspoon cinnamon
½ teaspoon cloves
1 teaspoon nutmeg
1 cup raisins
1 cup chopped nuts

Combine flour, baking powder and spices. Dissolve soda in tomato soup. Cream shortening and sugar. Add tomato soup with soda and sifted dry ingredients. Stir in raisins and nuts. Place into greased and floured loaf pan. Bake at 350 degrees for 1 hour.

Frosting:
¼ pound cream cheese
1½ cups powdered sugar
1 teaspoon vanilla

MARION (LORENZ) KAUFFMAN
submitted by KAROLYN (KAUFMAN) ZERGER A'46, x'50

DATE PUDDING

1 cup sugar
½ cup milk
1 cup flour
1 teaspoon baking powder
⅛ teaspoon salt
1 cup dates, cut into pieces
1 cup broken nutmeats
1 cup brown sugar
1 tablespoon butter
2 cups boiling water

Mix first 7 ingredients; pour batter into buttered 8x8-inch pan. Combine remaining ingredients; pour over batter in pan. Bake at 350 degrees for 25 minutes.

While I was a resident at Haury Hall during my years at Bethel, it was customary to have hall meetings every Monday evening at 10:30 (the weekday curfew at the time). One time when it was my turn to furnish treats, my mother delivered (from 15 miles away) this delicious dessert, still warm from the oven.

CAROL (REIMER) DUERKSEN '68

HOMEMADE SWEETENED CONDENSED MILK

1 cup instant nonfat dry milk
⅔ cup sugar
⅓ cup boiling water
3 tablespoons margarine

Combine ingredients in blender. Blend until smooth. The recipe makes 1¼ cups or the equivalent of 1 can. To thicken, let mixture sit in refrigerator for 24 hours.

LOUISE (DUERKSEN) KOEHN '44, faculty

CRANBERRY BREAD

2 cups flour	1 orange, juiced
1 cup sugar	2 tablespoons melted oleo
1½ teaspoons baking powder	water
½ teaspoon salt	1 egg, beaten
½ teaspoon soda	1 cup whole cranberries
	1 cup walnuts

Sift dry ingredients together. Combine orange juice, oleo and enough water to make ¾ cup. Add egg, then cranberries and walnuts. Bake in greased loaf pan for 1 hour at 325 degrees.

This recipe was given to me by Mrs. Howard Stutzman, along with a loaf of cranberry bread decorated with holly and berries, at Christmastime in 1955 when we lived in the trailer park on East 23rd Street in North Newton. Each Christmas as I make and give gifts of this cranberry bread I am reminded of her, of living in a 23-foot-long trailer and using a community bathroom and laundry facilities.

MARIAN (KLEINSASSER) TOWNE '55

PEARL TAPIOCA

3 tablespoons pearl tapioca	½ cup sugar
1 quart milk, scalded	pinch of salt
2 eggs, beaten	

Soak pearl tapioca in warm water overnight. Drain. Combine milk, beaten eggs, sugar, salt and soaked tapioca. Cook until it thickens.

This was served during the 1920s and 1930s. The students nicknamed it "freshman tears" or "fish eyes."

EDNA (RAMSEYER) KAUFMAN faculty

TURKEY SPREAD

2 cups cooked or leftover turkey
1 small can water chestnuts
1 teaspoon curry powder
½ teaspoon salt
½ cup salad dressing

Grind together turkey and water chestnuts; add remaining ingredients. Spread on favorite bread.

\Note: Ground turkey and water chestnuts freeze well. Add dressing and spices when thawed.

LOUISE (DUERKSEN) KOEHN '44, faculty

CHU PAO PA (Chinese Meat Dumplings)

Dough:
1½ cups flour
½ egg, beaten
warm water

Sift flour on board and add beaten egg and enough water to make a stiff dough. Knead until smooth and let stand 7-8 minutes before rolling. Roll very thin and cut into round pieces to cover meatballs the size of a walnut.

Filling:
½ pound chopped beef
1 tablespoon chopped pork
1 tablespoon chopped mushrooms
1 tablespoon bamboo sprouts
1 teaspoon chopped onion
1 teaspoon soy sauce
dash of pepper
1 pint beef stock

Mix chopped ingredients. Add soy sauce and dash of pepper. Shape into balls and cover each with a thin round piece of dough. Pinch edges together and steam a few at a time for 30 minutes over beef stock. Serve immediately with a hot oil and vinegar sauce for dipping (mixture of white vinegar and Chinese hot oil).

HAZEL S. (DESTER) KAUFMAN A'16
submitted by KIRSTEN L. ZERGER '73

SÜ FEN (Chinese)

1½ cups dry sü fen, soaked in boiling water for 3 hours
3 tablespoons oil
1 cup raw beef, diced fine
1 teaspoon cornstarch
½ cup fresh mushrooms, chopped
1½ cups beef stock
1-2 teaspoons fresh ginger root, finely chopped
2 large cloves fresh garlic, crushed
½ teaspoon red pepper
salt

Put soaked sü fen into hot frying pan with oil; let it heat thoroughly. Add beef, mushrooms and all other seasonings; adjust seasonings for flavor and "hotness." When beef has changed color, add beef stock. After it boils, add a bit of cornstarch to thicken to a thin gravy. Serve immediately.

This dish is spicy and hot, and so good!

HAZEL S. (DESTER) KAUFMAN A'16
submitted by KIRSTEN L. ZERGER '73

TOMATO CHUTNEY (Indian)

chopped tomatoes	salt
onions	black pepper
bananas (optional)	lemon juice

Another tomato chutney:
4 fresh tomatoes, chopped
1 large can whole tomatoes, chopped
½ gram sweet pepper, chopped
a bit of fresh parsley
chopped onion
dash of cayenne pepper
lemon juice
black pepper
salt

Various chutneys are on the market.

SELMA (DICK) UNRUH x'43, staff

DAHL (Split Green Peas or Lentils)

½ pound split peas
salt
3-4 cups water
lemon juice
chopped onion (optional)

Cook 10 minutes at 10 pounds pressure. Allow to cool normally. Add additional water (thick gravy consistency) and about 2 tablespoons lemon juice. Garnish with browned chopped onion, if desired.

SELMA (DICK) UNRUH x'43, staff

INDIAN BREAD

2 cups whole wheat flour
1 cup white flour
1 teaspoon salt
1 tablespoon shortening
1 cup milk

Knead to a spongy consistency (when pressed it will spring back). Roll out thin, cut into circles and fry in deep fat. If the temperature is right, both sides will bulge when fried. *This is good also with jam.*

SELMA (DICK) UNRUH x'43, staff

RICE

Bring water (1½ cups water to 1 cup rice), salt and 1 tablespoon oleo to a boil. Add rinsed rice, cover, turn heat down. Cook 20 minutes; remove from heat. Set aside until ready to use.

Variation for rice: Brown ½ cup chopped onion, ½ teaspoon garlic powder, 1 teaspoon turmeric in ½ cup oleo. Remove onion and use for garnish. Add rice to oleo and garlic mixture. Garnish with browned onions, peanuts and raisins, if desired.

SELMA (DICK) UNRUH x'43, staff

JAMBALAYA (African)

½ pound bacon, diced
2 cups canned tomatoes
1 cube beef bouillon
¼ teaspoon black pepper
1 cucumber, peeled
    and halved
1½ cups celery
1½ pounds shrimp
4-5 onions
2 cups water
1 teaspoon salt
1 cup brown or wild rice
½ cup celery leaves
2 green peppers, diced

Cook bacon in large pan until fat flows. Add onions; brown. Add tomatoes, water, cucumber and seasonings. When boiling, add rice. Cook for 30 minutes. *I cook it slowly for 2 hours.* Add remainder of vegetables and simmer for 10 minutes. Add shrimp and just heat.

My version of Jambalaya: Lightly sauté celery and peppers in butter. Remove celery leaves and halved cucumber from rice mixture. Combine rice mixture, celery, peppers and shrimp; bring just to a boil. Cut 2 tomatoes into 1-inch chunks and scatter through and on top of serving dish. This recipe serves 8 generously.

GREGORY J. STUCKY '71

TURKISH-STYLE ROAST LEG OF LAMB

3 tablespoons grated ginger root
2 cloves crushed garlic
2 tablespoons strained lime juice
½ cup unflavored yogurt
1½ teaspoons salt
½ teaspoon freshly ground black pepper
1 tablespoon ground coriander
½ teaspoon ground cloves
½ teaspoon ground cinnamon
½ teaspoon ground cardamom

In small bowl, combine ginger, garlic, lime juice, yogurt, salt and pepper. Blend well. With sharp knife, trim lamb of as much fat as possible. Score crosshatches ¼-inch deep across meat surface as if preparing ham for glazing. Place lamb on platter and brush yogurt marinade generously over entire surface. Allow lamb to marinate 3-12 hours; if over 3 hours, cover loosely with plastic wrap and refrigerate until 2 hours before final preparation. Allow 1½ hours for final preparation.

In small skillet, combine coriander, cloves, cinnamon and cardamom. Toast, stirring frequently, over moderate to low heat until spices start to darken, about 3-4 minutes. Set aside to cool.

Remove plastic wrap from lamb and transfer it to roasting pan. With a teaspoon, sprinkle toasted spices over lamb's surface. The lamb may be roasted in 350-degree oven or on a charcoal grill. *We prefer the latter method for its extra taste.* Calculate the lamb's roasting time based on its weight before fat was trimmed off as follows: 11 minutes per pound for rare, 14 minutes for medium to well-done. (The times may seem short, but lamb will be overcooked if traditional roasting times are followed.) Roast undisturbed. Transfer meat to serving platter and let rest 15 minutes before carving. Meanwhile, boil remaining roasting juices in pan over high heat until reduced by one-third. Serve in gravy boat as a sauce with the lamb.

This Greek Easter meal is a family tradition.

DAVID W. KAUFMAN '73

ENCHILADA CASSEROLE (Mexican)

1-2 pounds ground
    beef, fried
large can refried beans
large can tomatoes
1 can tomato paste
1 can water (or less)
2 cans green chili (or
    less)
1 can enchilada sauce
grated cheese
12 corn tortillas,
    crushed

Mix first 7 ingredients with grated cheese. Scatter crushed tortillas on top. Bake at 300 degrees for 45 minutes (or 375 degrees for 30-40 minutes).

For a double recipe, use 2 cans green chili (diced), 1 can hot enchilada sauce and 1 can mild enchilada sauce. *I serve sour cream and mashed avocado as side condiments.*

LOIS (FRANZ) BARTEL '60

NAVAJO TACOS (American Indian)

3 cups flour	1 tablespoon shortening
4 teaspoons baking powder	1 egg, beaten
1 teaspoon salt	warm water to make
½ cup powdered milk	1⅓ cups

Mix together flour, baking powder, salt, powdered milk and shortening. Add egg and water mixture all at once. Knead thoroughly. Cover and let rise 45 minutes or longer. Pinch off dough the size of a bun. Flatten into a round circle. Deep-fry in hot oil (425 degrees). Push dough into oil so it gets light and fluffy. Remove when both sides are nice and brown. Serve with topping made of:

1½ pounds ground beef, browned and fat removed

1 package taco seasoning

¾ cup water

Simmer 15 minutes. Add 1 large can of refried beans. Heat thoroughly. To serve, place fried bread on plate. Cover with topping. Add chopped onion, shredded lettuce, diced tomatoes and grated cheese. Pass bottle of taco sauce for those who like it hot. *Delicious!*

For many years we were teachers in a public school on the Navajo reservation at Ganado, Arizona.

DELLA (WALTNER) KLASSEN '43

BOBOTIE (South African Ground Beef Casserole)

2 pounds ground beef	10 dried apricots
1 large onion	1 teaspoon curry powder
2 tablespoons butter or oil	12 almonds, quartered
1 thick slice bread	½ teaspoon salt
1 cup milk	¼ teaspoon pepper
1 tablespoon apricot jam	6 bay leaves
2 tablespoons lemon juice	2 eggs
⅓ cup raisins	

Sauté onion in butter or oil. Soak bread in half of milk. Mix all other ingredients *except eggs*. Spoon into baking dish. Beat milk and soaked bread with eggs, pour over meat mixture. Bake about 45 minutes in medium oven. Serve with rice, chutney, coconut and chopped nuts.

MELVA (GOERING) WIEBE '47

BAKLAWA (Arabic) BAKLAVA (Greek)

1 pound baklawa dough (fillo dough purchased at delicatessens)

1 cup melted clarified butter (see below)

2 cups chopped walnuts

1 cup chopped almonds

½ cup sugar

¼ teaspoon cinnamon

¼ teaspoon nutmeg

Syrup:

1⅓ cups sugar	1 stick cinnamon
¾ cup honey	2 slices orange
½ cup water	2 slices lemon

Combine syrup ingredients; simmer 10 minutes. Cool.

Unfold dough. Cover with damp cloth to prevent drying. Brush 10x15-inch pan with melted clarified butter. Put layer of dough in pan and butter lightly. (If dough is too wide, cut to fit or fold in edges; any size of pan can be used.) Add 2 layers of dough; butter the second. Continue until half the dough is used, about 12 layers.

Mix nuts, sugar, cinnamon and nutmeg; spread over dough. Arrange remaining dough on top, buttering alternate layers. Do not butter top layer until it has been cut with a very sharp knife into diamond shapes. (Cut through only 1 or 2 layers.) Cut vertical lines 1½ inches apart, then cut diagonally. Butter each piece well. Bake in preheated 250-degree oven about 1½ hours until puffed and very light brown. Pour cooled syrup over hot baklawa. Store and serve at room temperature.

Clarified butter:

Simmer butter 20 minutes. Remove from heat and let rest several minutes. Skim foam from top and carefully pour off clear butter, allowing impurities to remain at bottom of pan.

CLARA (FRANZ) REIMER '48

NIGERIAN CHICKEN

2 tablespoons salad oil	⅓ cup tomato paste
1 medium onion, chopped	2 teaspoons salt
3-3½-pound broiling chicken, cut up	¾ cup water

In Dutch oven or large skillet, over medium high heat, cook onion in salad oil until golden. Add chicken, tomato paste, salt and water. Cook, covered, over low heat 1½ hours or until chicken is fork-tender, basting occasionally. Serve with joloff rice (see below).

MARTHA M. (FRIESEN) GRABER '41

JOLOFF RICE (Nigerian)

2 tablespoons salad oil	⅓ cup tomato paste
2 medium onions, chopped coarsely	1¼ teaspoons salt
1½ cups water	¼ teaspoon thyme leaves
3 medium tomatoes, cut in chunks	⅛ teaspoon cayenne pepper
	1 cup long-grain rice

In large saucepan, over medium-high heat, cook onions in salad oil until golden. Add remaining ingredients, except rice, and cook 10 minutes. Add rice. Cover pan and cook over low heat 25-30 minutes until rice is tender. Stir as needed. Serves 6.

MARTHA M. (FRIESEN) GRABER '41

LIBYAN MEAT SAUCE (for Cous Cous)

1½ pounds lamb or beef, cut into 2-inch squares
¼ cup olive oil
2 large onions (1 chopped, 1 sliced)
1 large tomato, cut in slices
1 teaspoon crushed red pepper (adjusted to taste)
½ teaspoon ground allspice
2 teaspoons turmeric
2 teaspoons salt
12 ounces tomato paste
3 cups water
4 medium potatoes, peeled and quartered
16-ounce can chick peas (garbanzo beans)

Brown meat in oil. Add chopped onion and tomato; cook 10 minutes. Add red pepper, allspice, turmeric, salt, tomato paste and water. Cover and simmer 1 hour. Add potatoes and sliced onion (½-inch slices). Simmer 30 minutes. Add more water if needed. Add chick peas; simmer 10 minutes or until hot. Serve over 1 pound cous cous (pre-cooked bulgar-type wheat, or rice), steamed and salted lightly.

MARTHA M. (FRIESEN) GRABER '41

CURRANT SCONES (English)

1 cup flour
3 tablespoons sugar
2 teaspoons baking powder
½ teaspoon salt
⅓ cup shortening
½ cup oatmeal
½ cup currants
2 eggs, beaten

Cut shortening into mixed dry ingredients. Stir in oatmeal and currants. Add eggs and stir. Knead 10 times on lightly floured board. Pat into 7-inch circle; cut into 8 wedges. Place on ungreased pan. Bake 8 minutes in 450-degree oven.

We have served tea and scones to many students in our home. They are a favorite of our family. We learned to enjoy them during our sabbaticals in England. They are best served fresh and warm with butter.

ALDINE (SLAGELL) SPRUNGER staff

SCONES WITH YEAST (English)

1 tablespoon yeast
5 ounces warm water
5¼ cups white flour
6 tablespoons butter
2 tablespoons baking powder
1 egg
½ cup sugar
⅓ cup milk
1 cup sultanas (currants, golden raisins)

Dissolve yeast in water and stir in ¾ cup flour; set in warm place for 30 minutes. Sift remaining flour and baking powder into bowl; cut in butter. Add remaining ingredients except sultanas. Mix vigorously to a smooth dough; knead in the sultanas. Shape dough into a ball; pat or roll to 1-inch thickness. Cut into 2-inch rounds and place on greased cookie sheet. Cover with plastic wrap and let rise 40 minutes. Brush with milk after 30 minutes. Bake in 450 degree oven for 12-15 minutes. Cool on wire rack.

Adapted to U.S. ingredients and measurements from The Sainsbury Book of Teatime Favorites. *Sainsbury is a large grocery chain in England.*

ALDINE (SLAGELL) SPRUNGER staff

HOPI FRY BREAD (American Indian)

4 cups flour
4 teaspoons baking powder
1 teaspoon salt
1⅓-1½ cups water, approximately
shortening for frying

In large bowl, mix flour, baking powder and salt. With a fork, gradually stir in just enough water to make a soft dough. Continue stirring until all flour has been absorbed. Cover bowl with clean towel; set aside for 30 minutes. Shape dough into 16 balls, each about the size of a small egg. (If dough is too sticky to handle, knead briefly on heavily floured board, sprinkling on additional flour as needed.) With floured rolling pin, shape each ball on lightly floured board into a disk about 4 inches in diameter and ½-inch thick.

Heat 1½ inches of shortening in heavy frying pan until it is just about to smoke. Fry 3-4 pieces of bread at a time in hot fat until they are puffy and browned on both sides. Drain fry bread on paper towels and continue frying until all of the bread is done. Serves 6 to 8.

EDNA (KLIEWER) LINSCHEID x'32

PILAU (African)

2 pounds goat or beef, cubed
1 chopped onion
1 tablespoon ground cumin
½ teaspoon cinnamon
½ teaspoon ground cardamom
10 crushed garlic cloves
2 tablespoons tomato paste
2 cups rice
4 cups water
1 teaspoon salt

Cook onion until tender. Add meat and tomato paste; cook until meat is tender. Add remaining ingredients and simmer until rice is tender. Serve with raw onion slices, lemon wedges and green hot peppers.

Pilau is the most common celebration main dish served in northeastern Kenya. It is served on large platters and placed on the floor where segregated groups eat it with their right hands. Somalis spend most of their social time sitting on woven mats, so this is where their eating takes place also.

KAREN (KLASSEN) HARDER '79

SOMALI CHAI (African)

10 cloves
8 cardamom pods, crushed
1/2 teaspoon ground ginger
4 cups water
2 cups milk
1 tablespoon loose tea leaves
3/4 cup sugar

Combine ingredients and heat to boiling; simmer 5 minutes. Strain and serve.

This type of tea is served in a Somali household at all times of the day. The woman of the house makes a large batch in the morning over a charcoal or wood fire. It is then stored in thermos containers. When it is available, the Somalis prefer to make the tea using smoked camel's milk.

KAREN (KLASSEN) HARDER '79

TOSTONES (Caribbean)

2 green plantains
cooking oil
salt

Peel and slice plantains very thin. Fry in hot oil at least 1-inch deep until crisp. Drain on absorbent paper toweling. Sprinkle with salt.

These are like potato chips, but with a flavor all their own. They can be made beforehand and kept in an airtight container; however, they are tastiest when freshly made.

LAURA (GOERING) KREHBIEL x'43

EMPANADAS (South American)

pastry for 2 two-crust pies
1 tablespoon butter
1/3 cup chopped onion
1/2 cup peeled chopped tomatoes
1/4 cup chopped green pepper
1/2 pound lean ground beef
3/4 teaspoon salt
1/8 teaspoon pepper
few drops Tabasco sauce
1 hard-boiled egg, chopped
1/4 cup green olives, chopped

Melt butter in skillet; add onion, tomatoes and green pepper. Cook over low heat until onion is soft. Stir in beef; cook until no pink remains. Remove from heat and stir in remaining ingredients. Cool. Roll out pastry. Cut into 4-inch rounds. Place 1 tablespoon filling in center of each round. Brush edges with water and fold dough in half, pressing edges together firmly. Cut steam vent in top of each. Bake in hot oven (425 degrees) until lightly browned, about 15 minutes. Makes about 2½ dozen.

SARA ORTIZ

SWEET 'N SOUR MEATBALLS

1 pound ground pork
2 tablespoons minced onion
2 tablespoons green pepper
1½ teaspoons dry mustard
1 teaspoon chili powder
1 teaspoon salt
1/4 teaspoon pepper
1/2 cup milk
1 egg, beaten

Mix all ingredients. Form into small balls which may be frozen for later use, or proceed to brown and serve with sauce:

2/3 cup brown sugar
2 tablespoons cornstarch
2 teaspoons dry mustard
1/2 cup vinegar
1/2 cup catsup
1/4 cup chopped onion
2 tablespoons soy sauce
1 cup crushed pineapple, undrained
1/2 cup water

Cook until thick and glossy. Pour over meatballs; simmer for 20 minutes or bake 30 minutes at 350 degrees.

DELORES (FREY) FUNK x'62

PEANUT BUTTER MEATBALLS

1/2 cup peanut butter
1/2 pound ground beef
1/4 cup finely-chopped onion
2 tablespoons chili sauce
1 teaspoon salt
1/8 teaspoon pepper
1 egg, beaten
2 tablespoons peanut oil
2 cups seasoned tomato sauce

Mix peanut butter lightly with beef, onion, chili sauce, salt, pepper and egg. Form into 12 meatballs. Brown in hot peanut oil. Add tomato sauce; cover and simmer about 30 minutes. Serve with cooked rice or spaghetti. Yields 4 servings.

ADELLA (NIKKEL) HARMON '57

BEST POT ROAST

4-pound roast
1 package dry onion soup mix
1 can cream of mushroom soup

Place roast in heavy foil. Cover with soups. Fold foil around roast; bake in slow oven (325 degrees) until tender, about 2½-3 hours. This makes a ready-to-serve gravy.

If you are looking for a tasty meat, calling for little effort, time or preparation, this is it.

GLADYS (GRABER) GOERING '40

BOLOGNA

2 pounds ground beef
1 cup water
1½ teaspoons liquid smoke
2 tablespoons meat tenderizer
¼ teaspoon onion powder
⅛ teaspoon salt
¼ teaspoon garlic powder
1½ teaspoon crushed peppercorns
1 tablespoon mustard seeds

Mix all ingredients; form into 3 rolls. Wrap in plastic wrap (do not use foil); refrigerate 24 hours. Remove wrap; place on boiler pan or pan with rack. Bake 1 hour and 45 minutes at 300 degrees. Cool. Rewrap and refrigerate or freeze.

The Saturday evening meal at the dining hall usually consisted of bologna and cold cuts, baked beans, chips and homemade pie.

BONNIE R. (FRANZ) EPP '68

JAKE'S FAVORITE CRAB DISH

1 pound crab meat
6 hard-boiled eggs, chopped fine
3 tablespoons onions, chopped
3 tablespoons green peppers, chopped
¼ teaspoon salt
2½ cups mayonnaise
2½ cups milk
12 slices white bread, crusts removed
grated cheddar cheese
cornflakes, crushed

In 3-quart casserole, mix mayonnaise and milk. Add remaining ingredients; mix well. Cover with grated cheese. Refrigerate overnight. Remove 1 hour before baking. Sprinkle crushed cornflakes on top of cheese. Bake 45 minutes at 325 degrees.

BETH (ELDRIDGE) GOERING '40

FONDUE PARTY

Cut 2 pounds beef tenderloin into 1-inch cubes. Refrigerate this while making the sauces. Serves 4. *We like to serve at least three sauces.*

HORSERADISH SAUCE

1 cup sour cream
2 tablespoons horseradish
½ teaspoon lemon juice
¼ teaspoon Worcestershire sauce
⅛ teaspoon salt

Combine; refrigerate. Makes 1 cup.

BLUE CHEESE SAUCE

½ cup sour cream
¼ cup crumbled blue cheese
1 teaspoon Worcestershire sauce
¼ teaspoon salt

Combine; refrigerate. Makes ¾ cup.

HOT 'N SPICY SAUCE

1 cup chili sauce
½ cup chopped onion
3 tablespoons lemon juice
2 tablespoons salad oil
1 teaspoon brown sugar
2 teaspoons vinegar
1 clove garlic, crushed
½ teaspoon Tabasco sauce
¼ teaspoon dry mustard
¼ teaspoon salt

Combine all ingredients in small saucepan. Heat to boiling; simmer 5 minutes. Serve warm or cool. Makes 1¼ cups. About 15 minutes before dinner, mound meat on bed of greens. Measure enough salad oil to fill a depth of 1½-2 inches in fondue pot. Pour into pan and heat on stove until a bread cube will brown in 1 minute. Carefully pour hot oil into fondue pot and light burner under pot. Place in middle of table. Pass meat and sauces so guests can put some on their plates.

To eat beef fondue, spear a cube of beef with long-handled fork, dip into hot oil and cook until crusty on outside, juicy and rare inside. Dip cooked meat into sauce of your choice.

This is good served with a tossed salad and rolls, and fruit for dessert.

HELEN (VORAN) VOTH x'46

SPAGHETTI SAUCE

1 pound ground beef
1 package spaghetti sauce mix
6-ounce can tomato sauce
16-ounce can spaghetti sauce with mushrooms

Follow directions on sauce mix package. Add tomato and spaghetti sauces; blend. Heat to a simmer. Brown ground beef; remove excess fat. Add to sauce mixture and simmer, stirring occasionally. Cook spaghetti according to package directions.

JANET M. (KLAASSEN) VOTH '63
ORVIN E. VOTH '64, faculty

We began inviting college students to our home in 1975 when there were 45 students we knew on campus as a result of my teaching and our role as youth fellowship sponsors at the college church. That first year, each month we invited five students we knew and asked them each to bring a guest. More recently we have worked through the student services office and resident assistants in the dorms.

The evening always begins with a tour of our 100-year-old Victorian house (I do the tours; Orvin pours the sodas and cooks the spaghetti). Our house is known as the "spaghetti house" and I am known as the "spaghetti lady" when I call the dorms to invite another group of students.

JANET M. (KLASSEN) VOTH '63
ORVIN E. VOTH '64, faculty

SALMON SALAD

    2 cups chopped celery
    2 cups canned red salmon
    2 hard-boiled eggs, chopped
    2/3 cup mayonnaise

Mix and serve on lettuce bed with garnish of choice.

HELEN (JANZEN) HIRSCHLER x'11

Helen (Janzen) Hirschler, a Bethel student in 1907-08, recalls that salmon salad was the daily meal for her Bethel music teacher husband, Daniel A. Hirschler. After their wedding on July 1, 1909, they moved to Newton and set up housekeeping. She did not know the first thing about cooking, so she had to serve this salad, the only thing she could prepare. When her husband became ill, the doctor thought he had typhoid, but she said it was more likely due to her poor cooking! Mrs. Hirschler laughed as she recalled that Dan did not marry her for her domestic skills.

On another occasion she was designated to cook the Thanksgiving turkey for several families of guests from the East. She knew they liked their meat rare so she decided not to overbake the turkey. The eighteen-pound bird looked nice and brown until her husband began to carve it. The juice came out bright red. She had baked it about an hour. They ended up scraping off the outside meat to eat at the dinner; the remainder was quartered and baked several more hours.

MARIAM H. (PENNER) SCHMIDT '25, faculty

BOSTON CREAM PIE

    1/3 cup flour
    3/4 cup sugar
    1/4 teaspoon salt
    2 eggs, separated
    1 1/2 cups milk
    1/2 tablespoon butter
    1/2 teaspoon vanilla
    graham cracker pie shell, cinnamon-flavored

Mix dry ingredients. Combine slightly beaten egg yolks and milk; stir into dry ingredients. Add butter. Cook over low heat, stirring until thick. Fold in stiffly beaten egg whites and vanilla. Pour into shell; chill.

This is one of my favorite recipes from the home economics department.

LOLA M. HILL faculty
submitted by WINIFRED E. (REGIER) EWY '43

SCALLOPED CORN

    2 cups canned corn
    1 green pepper, minced
    1/2 cup buttered crumbs
    1 egg, well beaten
    1 cup medium white sauce
    1 teaspoon sugar

Combine white sauce and egg; beat thoroughly. Add corn, sugar and green pepper. Pour into well-oiled baking dish; cover with crumbs. Bake at 350 degrees until well-browned, about 30 minutes.

This is a recipe used in the 1930s.

LUCILLE J. (SCHROEDER) LEISY x'39

Thanksgiving Banquet
November 26, 1936, 6:30 p.m.

Menu

Fruit cup

Beef steak		*Mashed potatoes*
	Gravy	
Scalloped corn		*Buttered string beans*
Cranberry salad	*Olives*	*Pickles*
	Parkerhouse rolls	
Pumpkin pie		*Coffee*
Nuts		*Candies*

LUCILLE J. (SCHROEDER) LEISY x'39

BEET SALAD

    1 quart pickled beets
    3 medium-sized onions
    4 hard-boiled eggs
    1 cup salad dressing

Drain and dice beets, place in 2-quart mixing bowl. Dice onions and eggs; add to beets. Add salad dressing; mix well. Serve in bowl or on individual salad plates. Serves 8-10.

ETHEL (SCHINDLER) FAST '59

QUICK SPINACH SALAD

Salad:
    2 packages frozen spinach, chopped
    1/2 cup celery, chopped
    1/2 cup onions, chopped
    1 cup sharp cheese, shredded
    2 hard-boiled eggs, chopped

Dressing:
    2 teaspoons horseradish
    1/2 teaspoon salt
    2 teaspoons vinegar
    1 1/4 cups mayonnaise

Squeeze liquid out of thawed spinach; add next 4 ingredients. Make dressing at least a day before use. Toss into spinach when ready to serve. Makes 8 servings.

DIANE (KLASSEN) LEISY x'64

114

CHEESE DIP

1 can cream of mushroom soup
1-1½ pounds ground beef
¾ pound American cheese
1 can tomatoes with green chilies
½ cup green peppers, chopped fine
3 scallions or minced onions

Brown meat, pepper and scallions. Melt cheese; add meat mixture and all other ingredients. Serve hot.

RUTH (SCHROEDER) KOONTZ '43, staff

BAKED ZUCCHINI

4 zucchini, unpeeled and chopped
¼ cup salad oil
1 teaspoon salt
dash of pepper
garlic salt to taste
1 cup grated cheese
2 slices bread, cubed
1 small can evaporated milk
1 egg
¼ cup walnuts, chopped
Parmesan cheese

Combine zucchini, oil and seasonings with small amount of water; cook 10 minutes. Combine milk and egg; beat until blended. Pour over bread cubes; let stand until soaked. Place layers of zucchini, cheese, and bread mixture in greased 9-inch casserole. Bake at 350 degrees about 45 minutes. Serves 5-6. When nearly done, sprinkle Parmesan cheese and walnuts over the top.

MARGUERITE I. (GEIGER) FRETZ x'36

SPINACH SALAD

1 pound fresh spinach, washed and drained
      (or romaine, endive or leaf lettuce)
1 cup bean sprouts, drained
1 small can water chestnuts, drained and sliced
½ pound bacon, fried and crumbled
4 hard-boiled eggs, chopped
1 small onion, chopped

Toss with some of the following blender dressing:
¾ cup sugar
¼ cup salad oil
¼ cup vinegar
⅓ cup catsup
1 teaspoon Worcestershire sauce
2 teaspoons salt

MONICA (DIRKS) GROSS '45, staff

RECIPE INDEX

APPETIZERS
Cheese
    snacks. 35
    spread, Danish 105
Mushrooms, cheese-stuffed 105
Ryes, hot party 75
Salmon party log 105
Shrimp. 105
Tomato juice 81

BEVERAGES
Coffee punch. 75
Delta tea 32
Potassium pick-up 54

BREADS
Bread
    a man's wheat, oats 'n rye 2
    banana tea 75
    brown. 19
    cranberry 107
    honey whole grain 85
Buns
    hot cross. 103
    whole wheat. 87
Coffee cake
    dining hall. 33
    platz (fruit) 85
    yeast. 67
Muffins
    health 51
    raisin. 27
New Year's cookies
    pummelchen, Berliners, Bismarcks. 103
    Schmeckhaus 83
Rolls
    butterhorn. 50
    food processor whole wheat 82
    Parkerhouse 56

Zwieback
    Eunice (Unruh) Esau 86
    kleine (little) 59
    Wilma Toews 42

CAKES
Apple, Dutch 7
Chocolate, sour cream. 28
Crumb 16
Devil's food 66
Nellie Goertz 8
Rhubarb. 77
Tomato soup 106

CANDIES
Caramels, everyday vanilla 102
Chocolate coating 106
Coconut kisses. 15
Cremes, oriental 106
Fudge
    Boston cream 105
    carob fruit 105
Lollipops .102
Taffy, cold weather. 48
Toffee, English 15

COOKIES
Bars
    apricot 88
    O'Henry 38
Date wafers 1
Lebkuchen. 58
Lemon squares 32
Monster 91
Pan
    chocolate chip. 68
    oatmeal scotchie 101
Pecan. 3
Peppernuts (pfeffernuesse) 6
Rocks. 4
Tea. 50

116

DESSERTS

Apple crisp (or fruit crisp) 94
Blanc mange, plain 45
Chocolate marlowe 94
Condensed milk, homemade sweetened 106
Devil's food float 57
Fudge sauce, hot 25
Ice cream, Aunt Katie's 25
Icebox 46
Maple nut mold 21
Pudding
    date - Mildred (Haury) Brandt 44
    date - Carol (Reimer) Duerksen 106
    date - Lola M. Hill 40
    grapenut 34
    steamed 14
Rhubarb 9
Snowballs 89
Strawberry squares, frosty 47
Tapioca, pearl 107

INTERNATIONAL

African
    Bobotie (ground beef casserole) 109
    Jambalaya 108
    Libyan meat sauce (for cous cous) 110
    Nigerian chicken, joloff rice 109
    Pilau 110
    Somali chai 111
Arabic
    Baklawa .109
Caribbean
    Blue Mountain coffee chiffon 22
    Tostones 111
Chinese
    Chu pao pa (meat dumplings) 107
    Sü fen 107
English
    Scones
        currant 110
        with yeast 110
Greek
    Baklava 109
    Koulouraki (butter cookies) 84
Indian
    Bread 108
    Chutney, tomato 107
    Curry, chicken or beef 80
    Dahl (split peas or lentils) 108
    Rice 108

Indian, American
    Hopi fry bread 110
    Navajo tacos 109
Japanese
    Tempura 13
Mexican
    Enchilada casserole 108
South American
    Empanadas 111
    Plemanian suppe (little pocket soup) 78
Swiss
    Groguettli 58
Turkish
    Leg of lamb, roast 108

MAIN DISHES

Beef-lima skillet 23
Bierrocks, easy 93
Bubbat (sausage bread) 18
Casserole
    chicken 30
    country sausage 74
    top-of-stove meal 23
    tuna or chicken 26
Crepes, holiday Florentine 104
Eggs, goldenrod 21
Fondue party 112
    blue cheese sauce 112
    horseradish sauce 112
    hot 'n spicy sauce 112
Lasagna 90
Macaroni
    Ella's 43
    with cheese 29
Rice
    Chinese fried 22
    green chile, cheese bake 72
    Spanish 28
Soufflé, sure-fire cheese 4
Spaghetti
    crockpot 55
    sauce - Rita (Ewy) Ediger 55
    sauce - Janet (Klaassen) Voth 112
Spinach provencale 72
Stew, Spanish 99

MEATS

Bologna 112
Brisket, barbecued 81

Chicken
    barbecued, sauce for 97
    oven-fried 11
    scalloped 31
Crab dish, Jake's favorite 112
Ham, Virginia baked 52
Meatballs
    oven-barbecued 101
    peanut butter .111
    sweet 'n sour .111
Pork chops, cheesy baked 89
Ribs, sweet and sour 63
Roast
    beef 66
    best pot 111
Spareribs, barbecued 73
Steak, green pepper 98

PICKLES and RELISHES
Pickles
    dill 60
    okra 34
    stremel gurken (ripe cucumber strips) 3
    watermelon 7
Relish
    fresh vegetable 73
    triple service 41

PIES
Banana pecan 96
Black bottom 12
Boston cream 113
Chocolate cream 26
Cottage cheese apple 84
Oatmeal coconut 64
Zucchini 77

SALADS
Beet 113
Corn slaw 20
Cranberry gelatin 76

Macaroni 10
Rhubarb 17
Salmon 113
Spinach 114
    quick 113
Three-p 24

SANDWICHES
Burger
    bun, hot juicy 92
    hot 60
Cheese boxes 54
Tea 47
Turkey spread .107

SNACKS
Apples, daffy .100
Caramel corn, oven 95
Cheese charms 69
Dip
    cheese 114
    dill weed 95

SOUPS
Borscht
    beef 96
    beet 61
    chicken 61
Chili 37
Clam chowder 68
Lentil 70
Parsnip 18
Pflaumen-kielchen (cold fruit soup) 65
Steak 98

VEGETABLES
Beans, green 76
Corn, scalloped 113
Peas de luxe 17
Potatoes, peasant (bauern kartoffeln) 62
Zucchini, baked 114